# THE ENGLISH YEAR

THE ENGLISH YEAR

Summersdale Publishers Ltd
46 West Street
Chichester
West Sussex
PO19 1RP
UK

www.summersdale.com

Printed and bound by CPI Group (UK) Ltd, Croydon, CR0 4YY

ISBN: 978-1-84953-256-3

Substantial discounts on bulk quantities of Summersdale books are available to corporations, professional associations and other organisations. For details contact Summersdale Publishers by telephone: +44 (0) 1243 771107, fax: +44 (0) 1243 786300 or email: nicky@summersdale.com.

# THE ENGLISH YEAR

*A Literary Journey
through the Seasons*

PETER BUCKINGHAM

summersdale

# Contents

# Preface

*E*ngland is a great and ancient country, with a national character that has been – and continues to be – shaped by its ever-changing weather and gloriously diverse seasons. It could even be said that the ins and outs of the natural world are an English obsession: for instance, an Englishman will always be happy to resort to that most familiar of conversation-starters – 'What about this weather, eh?' – when unsure of what to say.

Throughout history the nation's best writers, including journalists, novelists, poets, politicians and even royalty, have penned their thoughts on the joys of summer, the splendour of autumn, the beauty of winter and the rejuvenation of spring, articulating their consternation and delight at the passing months and the unique conditions they bring.

Collected in this volume are insightful excerpts from the journals, letters and poems of some of England's favourite and most well-read literary figures, offering a window into their personal lives, but also into their thoughts and feelings about the land they made their home and the customs and practices they upheld. These are writings from a simpler, more peaceful time, before the hustle and bustle of modern life; a time that can be recaptured by experiencing a quiet dawn on the South Downs, by finding the time to tend the crops in one's vegetable patch or by following the simple traditions of Shrove Tuesday or May Day.

There is a saying that an Englishman's home is his castle, but in truth his home is just as much the rolling hills, wending rivers, farms, fields and villages of the countryside, or, for the urban dweller, his garden or local parks. And so it has been for hundreds of years.

From Samuel Pepys taking a stroll to St James's Park to play his flageolet in the sunshine, to William Cobbett's meanderings through the English countryside, observing and reporting on the life of rural people, to the American novelist Nathaniel Hawthorne's outsider's view on the native climate, each entry in this day-to-day journey through the seasons is a celebration of the always spellbinding, always captivating, English year.

# January

The frost-fires kindle, and soon
Over that sea of frozen foam
Floats the white moon.

WALTER DE LA MARE

I tell my secret? No indeed, not I:
Perhaps some day, who knows?
But not today; it froze, and blows, and snows,
And you're too curious: fie!
You want to hear it? well:
Only, my secret's mine, and I won't tell.

Or, after all, perhaps there's none:
Suppose there is no secret after all,
But only just my fun.
Today's a nipping day, a biting day;
In which one wants a shawl,
A veil, a cloak, and other wraps:
I cannot ope to every one who taps,
And let the draughts come whistling thro' my hall;
Come bounding and surrounding me,
Come buffeting, astounding me,
Nipping and clipping thro' my wraps and all.
I wear my mask for warmth: who ever shows
His nose to Russian snows
To be pecked at by every wind that blows?
You would not peck? I thank you for good will,
Believe, but leave that truth untested still.

Spring's an expansive time: yet I don't trust
March with its peck of dust,
Nor April with its rainbow-crowned brief showers,
Nor even May, whose flowers
One frost may wither thro' the sunless hours.
Perhaps some languid summer day,
When drowsy birds sing less and less,
And golden fruit is ripening to excess,
If there's not too much sun nor too much cloud,
And the warm wind is neither still nor loud,
Perhaps my secret I may say,
Or you may guess.

CHRISTINA ROSSETTI, 'WINTER: MY SECRET'

# January 1

I breakfasted, dined, supped & slept again at home. This morning very early about 1 o'clock a most dreadful Storm of Wind with Hail & Snow happened here and the Wind did not quite abate til the Evening. A little before 2 o'clock I got up, my bedsted rocking under me, and never in my Life that I know of, did I remember the Wind so high or of so long continuance. I expected every Moment that some Part or other of my House must have been blown down, but blessed be God the whole stood, only a few Tiles displaced.

James Woodforde (1779)

# January 2

Cold weather brings out upon the faces of people the written marks of their habits, vices, passions, and memories, as warmth brings out on paper a writing in sympathetic ink.

Thomas Hardy (1886)

# January 3

Night before last there was a fall of snow, about three or four inches, and, following it, a pretty hard frost. On the river, the vessels at anchor showed the snow along their yards, and on every ledge where it could lie. A blue sky and sunshine overhead, and apparently a clear atmosphere close at hand; but in the distance a mistiness became perceptible, obscuring the shores of the river, and making the vessels look dim and uncertain. The steamers were ploughing along, smoking their pipes through the frosty air... No such frost has been known in England these forty years!

Nathaniel Hawthorne (1854)

# January 4

I cannot quit Battle without observing, that the country is very pretty all about it. All hill, or valley. A great deal of wood-land, in which the underwood is generally very fine, though the oaks are not very fine, and a good deal covered with *moss*. This shows, that the clay ends before the *tap*-root of the oak gets as deep as it would go; for, when the clay goes the full depth, the oaks are always fine. The woods are too large and too near each other for hare-hunting; and, as to coursing it is out of the question here. But it is a fine country for shooting and for harbouring game of all sorts. It was rainy as I came home; but the woodmen were at work.

William Cobbett (1822)

# January 5

Thank you a thousand times, my dear friend, for your tender New Year's greeting and inquiries. I have passed well from 'under the saws and harrows' of the severe cold, and am better, both in apparent organic soundness and in strength for all occupation, than I once thought was possible for me.

George Eliot (1880)

# January 6

After dinner young Michell and I, it being an excellent frosty day to walk, did walk out, he showing me the baker's house in Pudding Lane, where the late great fire begun; and thence all along Thames Street, where I did view several places, and so up by London Wall, by Blackfriars, to Ludgate; and thence to Bridewell, which I find to have been heretofore an extraordinary good house, and a fine coming to it, before the house by the bridge was built; and so to look about St Bride's church and my father's house, and so walked home, and there supped together, and then Michell and Betty home, and I to my closet, there to read and agree upon my vows for next year, and so to bed and slept mighty well.

Samuel Pepys (1667)

# January 7

He dined with us on Friday, and I fear will not soon venture again, for the strength of our dinner was a boiled leg of mutton, underdone even for James; and Captain Foote has a particular dislike to underdone mutton; but he was so good-humoured and pleasant that I did not much mind his being starved.

Jane Austen (1807)

# January 8

Bushes and short trees blown like the flame of a candle. Long-tailed tits on dead stems of willow herb 4 ft. high. Rushes, half dead, half green.

Never go for a walk in the fields without seeing one thing at least however small to give me hope, the frond of a fern among dead leaves.

Richard Jefferies (1884)

## January 9

Ride to Brockenhurst – sudden snow-storm, careering between the trees and across the road like a charge of wild cavalry; wraps us in winter, clears off.

William Allingham (1866)

## January 10

The arum just appearing under the hedges as in April; and the Avens... has never lost its leaves but appears as green as at Spring.

John Clare (1825)

# January 11

Fierce frost still, but not very windy. The sun has scarce appeared for many days: so that the paths & roads have been hard & dry all day long. The Thames, it seems, is so frozen, that fairs have been kept on it; & the Ice has done great damage to the ships below bridge.

Covered the bulbs with straw, & the artichokes, & some of the most curious Asters: & put straw round the bloody wall-flowers. Lined the Cucumber bed a little: the plants look pretty well.

Gilbert White (1763)

# January 12

When I came out the night was superb. The sky was cloudless, the moon rode high and full in the deep blue vault and the evening star blazed in the west. The air was filled with the tolling and chiming of bells from St Paul's and Chippenham old Church. The night was soft and still and I walked up and down the drive several times before I could make up my mind to leave the wonderful beauty of the night and go indoors. To be alone out of doors on a still soft clear moonlit night is to me one of the greatest pleasures that this world can give.

Francis Kilvert (1873)

# January 13

As for the brain being useless after fifty, that is no general rule: witness the good and hard work that has been done in plenty after that age.

George Eliot (1862)

# January 14

How do you contrive to exist on your mountain in this rude season! Sure you must be become a snowball! As I was not in England in forty-one, I had no notion of such cold. The streets are abandoned; nothing appears in them: the Thames is almost as solid.

Horace Walpole (1760)

# January 15

This evening there was the most perfect and the brightest halo circling the roundest and brightest moon I ever beheld. So bright was the halo, so compact, so entire a circle, that it gave the whole of its area, and the moon itself included, the appearance of a solid opaque body, an enormous planet.

Samuel Taylor Coleridge (1805)

I

If seasons all were summers,
And leaves would never fall,
And hopping casement-comers
Were foodless not at all,
And fragile folk might be here
That white winds bid depart;
Then one I used to see here
Would warm my wasted heart!

II

One frail, who, bravely tilling
Long hours in gripping gusts,
Was mastered by their chilling,
And now his ploughshare rusts.
So savage winter catches
The breath of limber things,
And what I love he snatches,
And what I love not, brings.

THOMAS HARDY, 'THE FARM WOMAN'S WINTER'

# January 16

We leave dear Claremont, as usual, with the greatest regret; we are so peaceable here; Windsor is beautiful and comfortable, but it is a palace, and God knows how willingly I would always live with my beloved Albert and our children in the quiet and retirement of private life, and not be the constant object of observation, and of newspaper articles. The children (Pussette and Bertie) have been most remarkably well, and so have we, in spite of the very bad weather we had most days.

Queen Victoria (1844)

# January 17

It begun to be dark before we could come to Dartford, and to rain hard, and the horses to fayle, which was our great care to prevent, for fear of my Lord's displeasure, so here we sat up for to-night, as also Captains Cuttance and Blake, who came along with us.

Samuel Pepys (1661)

# January 18

The few days' severe weather ceased, and it became spring again. What a climate is ours!

Colonel Peter Hawker (1835)

# January 19

Went to A— Woods with S— and L— Saw a Barn Owl (*Strix flammea*) flying on broad daylight. At A— Woods, be it known, there is a steep cliff where we were all out climbing to inspect and find all the likely places for birds to build in, next spring.

W. N. P. Barbellion (1903)

# January 20

The season has continued uncommonly mild to this time. Many kinds of flowers are got above ground some weeks before their usual time: the snow-drops, & some Crocus's were in bloom before old December was out: & Farmer Knight complains that several of his turneps are in blossom. Covered the tulip, & Hyacinth-buds with a thin coat of tan that is rotten.

Have got some mould in excellent order for the early Cucumbers; it is a mixture of strong loam, ashes, & tan, tumbled about & well incorporated all the winter.

Gilbert White (1759)

# January 21

Walked on the hill-tops – a warm day. Sat under the firs in the park. The tops of the beeches of a brown-red, or crimson. Those oaks, fanned by the sea breeze, thick with feathery sea-green moss, as a grove not stripped of its leaves. Moss cups more proper than acorns for fairy goblets.

Dorothy Wordsworth (1798)

# January 22

On this day, which was very bright, the sun shone very warm on the Hot-bed from a quarter before nine, to three quarters after two. Very hard frost.

Gilbert White (1758)

# January 23

Went to meet of the Stag hounds. Saw a hind in the stream at L— with not a horse, hound, or man in sight. It looked quite unconcerned and did not seem to have been hunted. I tried to head it, but a confounded sheepdog got there before me and drove it off in the wrong direction... Got home at 6.30, after running and walking fifteen miles – tired out.

W. N. P. Barbellion (1904)

# January 24

Lymington. Fine and vernal. Ferry to steamer – delightful colours of earth, sky and sea, a bloom upon the landscape. From the Solent see the woody background of Lymington recede, the Island approach with a welcome; a boat with red sails passes in the sunshine. I feel tranquilly happy.

William Allingham (1867)

# January 25

How do you like this cold weather? I hope you have been earnestly praying for it as a salutary relief from the dreadfully mild and unhealthy season preceding it, fancying yourself half putrified from want of it, and that now you all draw into the fire, complain that you never felt such bitterness of cold before, that you are half starved, quite frozen, and wish the mild weather back again with all your hearts.

Jane Austen (1801)

# January 26

Had a Bottle of my Wine this evening in the B.C.R., being sconced for breaking Wind, while I was making Water in the Looking Glass, in the B.C.R.; by one Reynells. At Putt with Master won 0.0.1. The Frost is gone of, so it is all over with Skating.

James Woodforde (1762)

# January 27

This hotel, an immense place, built among picturesque broken rocks out in the blue sea, is quite delicious. There are bright green trees in the garden, and new peas a foot high. Our rooms are en suite, all commanding the sea, and each with two very large plate-glass windows. Everything good and well served.

Charles Dickens (1869)

# January 28

Out at night from nine till half-past one, and never heard or saw a bird, though a cold, frosty night, with a full moon and excellent tides.

Colonel Peter Hawker (1830)

# January 29

On this Day the mercury in the weather-glasses, which had been mounting leisurely for many days, we got one full degree above settled-fair in the parlour, & within half a degree of the same in the study.

My Father, who has been a nice observer of that up stairs for full 37 years, is certain that it never has been at that pitch before within that time.

Gilbert White (1758)

# January 30

Had a very indifferent Night of sleep scarce any at all. Recd of my Butcher for Tallow at 3d per lb 0.2.9. A Frost again but not so sharp as Yesterday. It did not freeze within doors last Night. Recd for Butter this Evening 1s 0d, 0.2.6. It froze also in the Afternoon, and the Barometer still rising, but in the Evening it thawed and some Rain fell. I was saying before dinner that there would be alteration of Weather soon as I a long time observed one of our Cats wash over both her ears – an old observation and now I must believe it to be a pretty true one.

James Woodforde (1794)

# January 31

A man that lives as I do, whose chief occupation, at this season of the year, is to walk ten times in a day from the fireside to his cucumber frame and back again, cannot shew his wisdom more, if he has any wisdom to shew, than by leaving the mysteries of government to the management of persons, in point of situation and information, much better qualified for the business.

William Cowper (1782)

Clouded with snow
The cold winds blow,
And shrill on leafless bough
The robin with its burning breast
Alone sings now.

The rayless sun,
Day's journey done,
Sheds its last ebbing light
On fields in leagues of beauty spread
Unearthly white.

Thick draws the dark,
And spark by spark,
The frost-fires kindle, and soon
Over that sea of frozen foam
Floats the white moon.

WALTER DE LA MARE, 'WINTER'

# February

One crocus is blown-out. Insects abound in the air:
bees gather much on the snow-drops, & winter-
aconites. Gossamer is seen, streaming from the
boughs of trees.

GILBERT WHITE

O Winter Sun!
How beautiful thy beams
Upon the chainèd earth!
The snows are melting and the gale
Is hushed; thou shinest, soft and pale,
O Winter Sun!
Upon a world that dreams,
And trembles with awakened hopes of birth.

O Joyful Green!
'Mid snowy patches gay
Thou peerest, and the sky
Shines blue through twiggèd boughs; each tree
Is aching now with thoughts of thee,
O Joyful Green!
Spring's heart is in the day
Though Winter's hands upon night's bosom lie.

LAURENCE ALMA-TADEMA, 'SUNSHINE IN FEBRUARY'

# February 1

Sowed 8 Succade-seeds.
The Cucumber-plants look finely.
   Frequent rains with a very high Barometre; & the Country in an unusual wet condition.

Gilbert White (1762)

# February 2

The coldest day within the memory of any man in Keyhaven. A gale from the north-east that no boat could 'row on end' in, and such a severely nipping frost that whatever was dipped in water became petrified in a few seconds. I walked out with the musket and sprung a mallard, and my hand was so benumbed that I absolutely lost the shot, from not having power in my thumb to cock the gun.

Colonel Peter Hawker (1830)

# February 3

Drank my morning draft at Harper's, and was told there that the soldiers were all quiet upon promise of pay. Thence to St James's Park, and walked there to my place for my flageolet and then played a little, it being a most pleasant morning and sunshine.

Samuel Pepys (1660)

# February 4

Walked a great part of the way to Stowey with Coleridge. The morning warm and sunny. The young lasses seen on the hill-tops, in the villages and roads, in their summer holiday clothes – pink petticoats and blue. Mothers with their children in arms, and the little ones that could just walk, tottering by their side. Midges or small flies spinning in the sunshine; the songs of the lark and redbreast; daisies upon the surf; the hazels in blossom; honeysuckles budding. I saw one solitary strawberry flower under a hedge. The furze gay with blossom. The moss rubbed from the pailings by the sheep, that leave locks of wool, and the red marks with which they are spotted, upon the wood.

Dorothy Wordsworth (1798)

# February 5

My poor Cow being rather better this morning, but not able to get up as yet, she having a Disorder which I never heard of before or any of our Somersett friends. It is called Tailshot, that is, a separation of some of the Joints of the Tail about a foot from the tip of the Tail, or rather a slipping of one Joint from another. It also makes all her Teeth quite loose in her head. The Cure, is to open that part of the Tail so slipt lengthways and put in an Onion boiled and some Salt, and bind it up with some coarse Tape.

James Woodforde (1790)

# February 6

The great titmouse, or sit ye down, sings.

One crocus is blown-out. Insects abound in the air: bees gather much on the snow-drops, & winter-aconites. Gossamer is seen, streaming from the boughs of trees.

Gilbert White (1790)

# February 7

G.R. – (who is a humorist) showed me his fowl-house, which was built of old-church-materials bought at Wellspring the builder's sale. R.'s chickens roost under the gilt-lettered Lord's Prayer and Creed, and the cock crows and flaps his wings against the Ten Commandments. It reminded me that I had seen these Ten Commandments, Lord's Prayer and Creed, before, forming the sides of the stone-mason's shed in the same builder's yard, and that he had remarked casually that they did not prevent the workmen 'cussing and damning' the same as ever.

Thomas Hardy (1878)

# February 8

A little practice on my flageolet, and afterwards walking in my yard to see my stock of pigeons, which begin now with the spring to breed very fast.

Samuel Pepys (1660)

# February 9

A very cold night and a slight shower of snow fell early this morning. Then it froze all day. The mountains all white... A grand night with stars glittering frosty keen and we came home at a rattling pace.

Francis Kilvert (1870)

# February 10

I have rested very well, and feel very comfortable to-day. What weather! I believe, however, the rain will cease.

Queen Victoria (1840)

# February 11

This I believe is as mild a time, considering the season of the year, as hath been known in the memory of man – everything having the appearance, and carrying with it the face of April, rather than of February (the bloom of trees only excepted); the meadows now are as verdant as sometimes they are in May, the birds chirping their melodious harmony, and the foot-walks dry and pleasant.

Thomas Turner (1759)

# February 12

Very fine. Walk, Efford Copse, first primroses; the Island, blue, sweet air, thrushes. Dine-out. Stars – from some bird a sudden single gush of song: a night-warbler?

William Allingham (1868)

## *Shrove Tuesday*

*While we were drinking, in comes Mr Day, a carpenter in Westminster, to tell me that it was Shrove Tuesday, and that I must go with him to their yearly Club upon this day, which I confess I had quite forgot. So I went to the Bell, where were Mr Eglin, Veezy, Vincent a butcher, one more, and Mr Tanner, with whom I played upon a viall, and he a viallin, after dinner, and were very merry, with a special good dinner, a leg of veal and bacon, two capons and sausages and fritters, with abundance of wine.*

Samuel Pepys (1660)

## February 13

It snowed a little this morning. Still at work at *The Pedlar*, altering and refitting. We did not walk, though it was a fine day. We received a present of eggs and milk from Janet Dockeray, and just before she went, the little boy from the Hill brought us a letter from Sara H., and one from the Frenchman in London.

Dorothy Wordsworth (1802)

Hope has her emblem, so has Love,
But I have vainly sought
For one, that might entirely prove
The picture of my thought.

If violets, when fresh with dew,
Could amaranthine be,
Their soothing, deep, and glowing hue
Would justly speak for me.

Or to some plant with tendrils fine,
With blossoms sweet and gay,
This office I would now assign;
But flowers will all decay!

A bird would suit my purpose more,
With filial heart endued;
But, ere their little life is o'er,
Birds lose their gratitude!

No emblem of the love I feel
Appears within my view;
Less ardent, or less pure the zeal,
Less tender, or less true!

All I can do is to avow,
My services are thine;
And that my spirit still shall bow,
Before my Valentine.

MARY MATILDA BETHAM, 'VALENTINE: FROM A YOUNG
LADY TO HER MOTHER'

# February 14

To-day I went for the first time into the kitchen garden on the Brobury side of the river. There was some old Espalier pears and apples and some young peach, nectarine and apricot trees against the walls, and one fine fig tree. The garden frames were in a very ruinous state.

Francis Kilvert (1878)

# February 15

We came here to settle yesterday – and also here Spring seems wonderfully forward! It can't last – and frost is sure to follow and cut off everything. At Windsor and Frogmore everything is budding – willow I see is green – rose-leaves out, and birds singing like in May!

Queen Victoria (1859)

# February 16

Early in the Morn' there was a small Frost but it thawed again fast about 8 o'clock after. I felt pretty well & strong this Morning. Dinner to-day, Shoulder of Mutton rosted &c. No News Papers &c. came to hand to day, Tho' my Butcher promised me faithfully to bring them which very much disconcerted me.

James Woodforde (1799)

# February 17

I dined at the Chaplain's Table with Pickering and Waring, upon a roasted Tongue and Udder, and we went on each of us for it 0.1.9 N.B. I shall not dine on a roasted Tongue & Udder again very soon.

James Woodforde (1763)

# February 18

Brimstone-coloured butterfly appears.
Large humble-bees.
Summer-weather.

Gilbert White (1779)

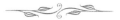

# February 19

The day was very cold, and the skaters seemed to enjoy themselves exceedingly. They were, I suppose, friends of the owners of the grounds, and Mr Bright said they were treated in a jolly way, with hot luncheons.

Nathaniel Hawthorne (1855)

# February 20

Yesterday I took a walk with my wife and two children to Bebbington Church. A beautifully sunny morning. My wife and U. attended church, J. and I continued our walk. When we were at a little distance from the church, the bells suddenly chimed out with a most cheerful sound, and sunny as the morning.

Nathaniel Hawthorne (1854)

# February 21

You must have had more snow at Goldmersham than we had here; on Wednesday morning there was a thin covering of it over the fields and roofs of the houses, but I do not think there was any left the next day. Everybody used to Southampton says that snow never lies more than twenty-four hours near it, and, from what we have observed ourselves, it is very true.

Jane Austen (1807)

# February 22

In the morning intended to have gone to Mr Crew's to borrow some money, but it raining I forbore, and went to my Lord's lodging and look that all things were well there.

Samuel Pepys (1660)

# February 23

Planted 14 Cuttings of the large, white Dutch-Currants (which I brought from Godalming) in the little Garden.

Gilbert White (1751)

# February 24

While the wind and dust continue to act the part they are now doing, I do not even wish to see you; for, I am sure, the less you expose yourself, the more likely you will be to receive the full effect of the mild weather when it comes.

Samuel Taylor Coleridge (1827)

# February 25

I am come hither for a little repose and air. The fatigue of a London winter, between Parliaments and rakery, is a little too much without interruption for an elderly personage, that verges towards – I won't say what... You know we have had an earthquake. Mr Chute's Francesco says, that a few evenings before it there was a bright cloud, which the mob called the bloody cloud; that he had been told there never were earthquakes in England, or else he should have known by that symptom that there would be one within a week. I am told that Sir Isaac Newton foretold a great alteration in Our climate in the year '50, and that he wished he could live to see it.

Horace Walpole (1750)

# February 26

A lovely warm morning so I set off to walk over the hills to Colva, taking my luncheon in my pocket, half a dozen biscuits, two apples and a small flask of wine. Took also a pocket book and opera glasses. Went on up the Green Lane. Very hot walking.

Francis Kilvert (1870)

# February 27

A walk and ride to Penjerrick, which looked eminently lovely basking in the sunshine.

Caroline Fox (1840)

# February 28

The last battalion of the Guards (Scots Fusiliers) embarked to-day. They passed through the courtyard here at seven o'clock this morning. We stood on the balcony to see them – the morning fine, the sun rising over the towers of old Westminster Abbey – and an immense crowd collected to see these fine men, and cheering them immensely as they with difficulty marched along. They formed line, presented arms, and then cheered us very heartily, and went off cheering. It was a touching and beautiful sight; many sorrowing friends were there, and one saw the shake of many a hand. My best wishes and prayers will be with them all...

Queen Victoria (1854)

# February 29

Very hard frost, & snow on the ground. The hot-bed goes-on but poorly: the plants don't grow, the snails damage them every night, & the succades don't come-up.

Gilbert White (1764)

Now in the dark of February rains,
Poor lovers of the sunshine, spring is born,
The earthy fields are full of hidden corn,
And March's violets bud along the lanes;

Therefore with joy believe in what remains.
And thou who dost not feel them, do not scorn
Our early songs for winter overworn,
And faith in God's handwriting on the plains.

'Hope' writes he, 'Love' in the first violet,
'Joy,' even from Heaven, in songs and winds and trees;
And having caught the happy words in these
While Nature labours with the letters yet,
Spring cannot cheat us, though her hopes be broken,
Nor leave us, for we know what God hath spoken.

GEORGE MACDONALD, 'IN FEBRUARY'

# *March*

Flesh and fleece, fur and feather,
Grass and green world all together;

GERARD MANLEY HOPKINS

Fair now is the springtide, now earth lies beholding
With the eyes of a lover the face of the sun;
Long lasteth the daylight, and hope is enfolding
The green-growing acres with increase begun.

Now sweet, sweet it is through the land to be straying
Mid the birds and the blossoms and the beasts of the field;
Love mingles with love, and no evil is weighing
On thy heart or mine, where all sorrow is healed.

WILLIAM MORRIS, FROM
'THE MESSAGE OF THE MARCH WIND'

# March 1

Great Dinners &c. given to day at the George Inn, viz, by Lord Ilchester, Lord Berkely of Bruton and Mr Mildmay, but neither were there. There were a great multitude of all Sorts, gentle and simple Mr Cox himself was there, Bells ringing &c. and a great Procession through Town with Musick playing & guns firing. They all came up in the Afternoon as far as Justice Creeds, and Mr Cox himself being back with him with the Procession down to the George Inn, where we drank success to him and was there for an Hour in the large Room with the multitude, till Mr Cox made a very handsome, sensible and genteel Speech, and then he withdrew, as did we immediately. Brother John dined, & spent the Evening with the Multitude.

James Woodforde (1768)

# March 2

Planted a plot in Turner's with five rows, three pints & half of early pease at four feet apart.

Very strong frost with thick ice: freezing air all day with flights of snow.

Gilbert White (1762)

# March 3

As I walked in the Churchyard this morning the fresh sweet sunny air was full of the singing of the birds and the brightness, and gladness of the Spring. Some of the graves were as white as snow with snowdrops.

Francis Kilvert (1878)

# March 4

Our excursion was most successful and gratifying. It rained very much all Monday evening at Portsmouth, but, nevertheless, we visited the *St Vincent* and the *Royal George* yacht, and the Prince went all over the Dockyards.

It stormed and rained all night, and rained when we set off on board the *Black Eagle* (the *Firebrand* that was) for Spithead on Tuesday morning; it, however, got quite fine when we got there, and we went on board the *Queen*, and a glorious sight it was; she is a magnificent ship, so wide and roomy, and though only just commissioned, in the best order. With marines, etc., her crew is near upon a thousand men! We saw the men at dinner, and tasted the grog and soup, which pleased them very much. Old Sir Edward Owen is very proud of her.

Queen Victoria (1842)

## March 5

I am glad that the myrtles reached you safe, but am persuaded from past experience that no management will keep them long alive in London, especially in the city... To give them, however, the best chance they can have, the lady must keep them well watered, giving them a moderate quantity in summer time every other day, and in winter about twice a week; not spring-water, for that would kill them.

William Cowper (1781)

## March 6

Sowed one melon-seed, from that curious Melon brought from Waverly in 1756, in each of the twelve pots. Bed heats well. Weather still stormy, & wet, that there is no removing the Cucumber-plants. It has rained of late from all Quarters of the Skie.

Gilbert White (1758)

# March 7

Here's a day! The ground covered with snow! What is to become of us? We were to have walked out early to near shops, and had the carriage for the more distant.

Jane Austen (1814)

# March 8

To-day there has come up from the country one of the spring gems of the year, a large bunch of the lilac Daphne, the old *Mezereum*. It is a small shrub, not a quick grower, and most people, especially gardeners, are afraid to cut it. But if this is done bravely at the time of flowering, I think it only grows stronger and flowers better the following year, and you get the benefit of the exceedingly fragrant blossoms.

Mrs C. W. Earle (1896)

# March 9

Very ill this morning, having had little or no Sleep all last Night, so very cold. A general Fast this Day. Mr Corbould read Prayers only this morning at Weston-Church. Mr Custance at Church, we were not. Mr Corbould called on us as he went to Church. Dinner to day, boiled Veal & Pork &c.

James Woodforde (1796)

# March 10

But, really, I feel so very happy among our English hedgerows, and find such inexhaustible and transcendent delight in the English flowers, and birds, and trees, and hills, and brooks, and, above all, in the wondrous sweet English faces and charming English ways, that nothing but a sense of duty will ever drive me to Rome and Venice.

John Smetham (1860)

# March 11

I must not forget what amazed us exceedingly in the night before, namely, a shining cloud in the air, in shape resembling a sword, the point reaching to the north; it was as bright as the moon, the rest of the sky being very serene, it being about eleven at night, and vanished not till above one, being seen by all the south of England.

John Evelyn (1643)

# March 12

Here it began to snow early in the morning and was snowing when we started at 10 o'clock for Regent Street, where K. had hired seats for the show; fortunately the snow just ceased falling a little before the Queen passed. How she and the Princess did shake their heads incessantly right and left, as if they had necks of India-rubber, and that for miles. The people were very enthusiastic, but the lack of sunshine took away all the splendour from the house-decorations and the helmets. The Princess looked large and imperial, I thought. People say that the accent is on the antepenultimate, Alexándrovna. If so, it rather spoils my chorus.

Alfred Tennyson (1874)

# March 13

One of the plants that was stopp'd down shows a Cucumber at the foot of a runner.

The sun in a few minutes scalded Part of a leaf that touch'd the Glass.

Gilbert White (1761)

# March 14

This night I went to Mr Creed's chamber where he gave me the former book of the proceedings in the fleet and the Seal. Then to Harper's where old Beard was and I took him by coach to my Lord's, but he was not at home, but afterwards I found him out at Sir H. Wright's. Thence by coach, it raining hard, to Mrs Jem, where I staid a while, and so home, and late in the night put up my things in a sea-chest that Mr Sheply lent me, and so to bed.

Samuel Pepys (1660)

# March 15

This day the weather, which of late has been very hot and fair, turns very wet and cold, and all the church time this afternoon it thundered mightily, which I have not heard a great while.

Samuel Pepys (1663)

The cock is crowing,
The stream is flowing,
The small birds twitter,
The lake doth glitter
The green field sleeps in the sun;
The oldest and youngest
Are at work with the strongest;
The cattle are grazing,
Their heads never raising;
There are forty feeding like one!

Like an army defeated
The snow hath retreated,
And now doth fare ill
On the top of the bare hill;
The plowboy is whooping anon-anon:
There's joy in the mountains;
There's life in the fountains;
Small clouds are sailing,
Blue sky prevailing;
The rain is over and gone!

WILLIAM WORDSWORTH, 'WRITTEN IN MARCH'

# March 16

A nice long gossiping breakfast visit from Dr Calvert. He has made up his mind to go to Penzance and see how it suits him. We shall miss him much.

Caroline Fox (1841)

# March 17

A turkey from Wargrave, the residence of my friend, and a turkey, as I conclude, of your breeding, stands a fair chance, in my account, to excel all other turkeys; and the ham, its companion, will be no less welcome.

William Cowper (1788)

# March 18

It was a bright cold afternoon and the March sun shining on the distant chalk downs made them look green and very near, only as if two or three miles away. After I had seen Dora home the beautiful clear fresh bright evening and the clear dry hard roads tempted me to go for a brisk solitary walk.

Francis Kilvert (1876)

# March 19

A very rainy morning. I went up into the lane to collect a few green mosses to make the chimney gay against my darling's return. Poor C., I did not wish for, or expect him, it rained so... Coleridge came in. His eyes were a little swollen with the wind. I was much stupefied. William came in soon after.

Dorothy Wordsworth (1802)

# March 20

He is a great botanist, so Anna Maria excited him about the luminous moss found in the cave at Argall; he informed us that the nature of all phosphoric lights is yet unknown, but it is generally believed to be an emission of light borrowed from the sun. We made a walking party to Pendennis Cavern, with which they were delighted.

Caroline Fox (1840)

# March 21

Great snow all the day, & most part of the night; which went off the next day in a stinking, wet fog. Very trying weather for Hot-beds, more like Jan than March. No sun for many Days.

Gilbert White (1758)

# March 22

Dry haze, groaning east wind, headache. I now believe the atmosphere with its changes has much more to do with health and spirits than I used to think possible. As we go in we find that many 'old-fashioned notions' have a good deal in them.

William Allingham (1864)

# March 23

One of the dear old bright happy mornings which seem peculiar and sacred to Whitney Rectory. The sun shone brightly in at the southern window bowered in roses and beautiful creeping plants and the birds chirped and sang in their bowers and I opened my eyes on the old familiar view as I looked up the valley of the Wye to the heights of Clyro Hill. Muirbach Hill dawned a soft azure through the tender morning mists.

Francis Kilvert (1874)

# March 24

Thank God! There's a sprinkle of sun to-day. The river to-night was low and the little walls and towers and chimneys on the opposite bank black against the night.

Katherine Mansfield (1914)

# March 25

I had two offers last night – not of marriage, but of music – which I find it impossible to resist. Mr Herbert Spencer proposed to take me on Thursday to hear 'William Tell', and Miss Parkes asked me to go with her to hear the 'Creation' on Friday. I have had so little music in this quarter, and these two things are so exactly what I should like, that I have determined to put off, for the sake of them, my other pleasure of seeing you.

George Eliot (1852)

Flesh and fleece, fur and feather,
Grass and green world all together;
Star-eyed strawberry-breasted
Throstle above her nested

Cluster of bugle blue eggs thin
Forms and warms the life within;
And bird and blossom swell
In sod or sheath or shell.

All things rising, all things sizing
Mary sees, sympathising
With that world of good,
Nature's motherhood.

Their magnifying of each its kind
With delight calls to mind
How she did in her stored
Magnify the Lord.

Well but there was more than this:
Spring's universal bliss
Much, had much to say
To offering Mary May.

GERARD MANLEY HOPKINS,
FROM 'THE MAY MAGNIFICAT'

# March 26

Very sharp Frosts of Nights still prevail and very cold Weather, no appearance of Spring yet to signify. The Wall fruit Trees seem to promise very well, the Apricots as full in Blossom as can be, but they are not full out, otherwise the Frost would cut them.

James Woodforde (1789)

# March 27

But as I work I feel the soothing of the angles of the sweet fields, and the peace of the tree-tops, and the comfort of love...

James Smetham (1863)

# March 28

It being an excessive wet and windy night, I had the opportunity, sure I should say the pleasure, or perhaps some might say the unspeakable happiness, to sit up with Molly Hicks, or my charmer, all night.

Thomas Turner (1765)

## March 29

Now the black Trees in the Regent's Park opposite are beginning to show green Buds; and Men come by with great Baskets of Flowers; Primroses, Hepaticas, Crocuses, great Daisies, etc., calling as they go, 'Growing, Growing, Growing! All the Glory going!' So my wife says she has heard them call: some old Street cry, no doubt, of which we have so few now remaining. It will almost make you smell them all the way from Calcutta. 'All the Glory going!'

Edward Fitzgerald (1857)

## *Good Friday*

*The English and Irish think it good to plant on this day, because it was the day when our Saviour's body was laid in the grave. Seeds, therefore, are certain to rise again.*

Nathaniel Hawthorne (1854)

# March 30

A lovely warm sunny morning, the purple plumes of the silver birch fast thickening with buds waved and swayed gently in the soft spring air against the deep cloudless blue sky. The apricot blossoms were blowing and under the silver weeping birch the daffodils were dancing and nodding their golden heads in the morning wind and sunshine.

Francis Kilvert (1876)

# March 31

It rained here hard yesterday in the morning, but cleared up about half-past twelve and was very fine indeed. Lord Melbourne went over to Brocket Hall and enjoyed it much.

Queen Victoria (1842)

See the land, her Easter keeping,
　　Rises as her Maker rose.
Seeds, so long in darkness sleeping,
　　Burst at last from winter snows.
Earth with heaven above rejoices;
　　Fields and gardens hail the spring;
Shaughs and woodlands ring with voices,
　　While the wild birds build and sing.

You, to whom your Maker granted
　　Powers to those sweet birds unknown,
Use the craft by God implanted;
　　Use the reason not your own.
Here, while heaven and earth rejoices,
　　Each his Easter tribute bring –
Work of fingers, chant of voices,
　　Like the birds who build and sing.

CHARLES KINGSLEY, 'EASTER WEEK'

# April

The heavens opened for the sunset to-night.
When I had thought the day folded and sealed,
came a burst of heavenly bright petals...

KATHERINE MANSFIELD

The sweetest thing, I thought
At one time, between earth and heaven
Was the first smile
When mist has been forgiven
And the sun has stolen out,
Peered, and resolved to shine at seven
On dabbled lengthening grasses,
Thick primroses and early leaves uneven,
When earth's breath, warm and humid, far surpasses
The richest oven's, and loudly rings 'cuckoo'
And sharply the nightingale's 'tsoo, tsoo, tsoo, tsoo':
To say 'God bless it' was all that I could do.

EDWARD THOMAS, FROM 'APRIL'

# April 1

Went this Morning early with Jenny to my Curacy at Babcary – where we breakfasted, dined, and spent the Afternoon. Captain Rooke and Sister Nanny dined & spent the Afternoon with us at Babcary. We had nothing but Bacon & Eggs for Dinner. There was an Eclipse of the Sun this Morning about nine o'clock, but it was nothing to what was expected by most People.

James Woodforde (1764)

# April 2

Spring has really arrived and even the grasshoppers are beginning to stridulate, yet Burke describes these little creatures as being 'loud and troublesome' and the chirp unpleasant. Like Samuel Johnson, he must have preferred brick walls to green hedges. Many people go for a walk and yet are unable to admire Nature simply because their power of observation is untrained.

W. N. P. Barbellion (1903)

## April 3

Made my great ten-light melon-bed with fifteen dung-carts of hot-dung. Laid an Hillock of Dorton-earth in the middle of each light; & cover'd the whole bed about two inches thick with earth. The earth wet & cloddy, & not in condition for the purpose. Supply'd the Artichoke-bed (which had lost most of it's plants) with very good slips from Dr Bristow's.

Gilbert White (1756)

## April 4

And I declare that the wonder of spring, so far from growing familiar, strikes upon the mind with a bewildering strangeness, a rapturous surprise, which is greater every year. Every spring I say to myself that I never realised before what a miraculous, what an astounding thing is the sudden conspiracy of tree and flowers, hatched so insensibly, and carried out so punctually, to leap into life and loveliness together.

A. C. Benson (1896)

# April 5

Sowed a Crop of leeks, beets, parsneps, turnep-radishes, & onions.

Unusual hot weather this week: during which, John, who was but a very young Gardener, scorch'd up, & suffocated all his forward Cucumbers: & drawed his melon-plants in the pots, but has not spoiled them.

Gilbert White (1757)

# April 6

Another lovely day for the whale; boats from all parts, and the Lymington steamer with a band of music. Went a second time, with General and Lady Elizabeth Thackery (who kindly invited me to take a passage in their boat), and took a sketch of the wonderful monster; and I cut out and brought home a few of the curious combings that are attached to his upper jaws, and which are the whalebones so general in use.

Colonel Peter Hawker (1842)

# April 7

The heavens opened for the sunset to-night. When I had thought the day folded and sealed, came a burst of heavenly bright petals... I sat behind the window, pricked with rain, and looked until that hard thing in my breast melted and broke into the smallest fountain, murmuring as aforetime, and I drank the sky and the whisper.

Katherine Mansfield (1914)

# April 8

You will deem it strange, but really some of the imagery of London has, since my return hither, been more present to my mind than that of this noble vale. I left Coleridge at seven o'clock on Sunday morning, and walked towards the city in a very thoughtful and melancholy state of mind. I had passed through Temple Bar and by St Dunstan's, noticing nothing, and entirely occupied with my own thoughts, when, looking up, I saw before me the avenue of Fleet Street, silent, empty, and pure white, with a sprinkling of new-fallen snow, not a cart or carriage to obstruct the view, no noise, only a few soundless and dusky foot-passengers, here and there.

William Wordsworth (1808)

## April 9

Walked to Stowey, a fine air in going, but very hot in returning. The sloe in blossom, the hawthorns green, the larches in the park changed from black to green in two or three days. Met Coleridge in returning.

Dorothy Wordsworth (1798)

# April 10

To Farringford by field-path, Miss T., Fitzjames S. and I – beautiful sunlit prospects, Yarmouth in the distance, gleaming river. They go in – I flee. Luncheon at Miss T.'s. We find A. T. and walk to the Beacon; meet one stranger, at sight of whom A. T. nearly turns back.

Lincolnshire stories. Preachers: 'Coom in your rags, coom in your filth, Jesus'll take ye, Jesus won't refuse ye.' 'Time has two ends, and the Law cooms down wi' a bang!' 'Glory' a very favourite word.

Lincolnshire manners. One of my brothers met a man in the lane near our house and said in a friendly voice, 'Good-night!' to which the man replied, 'Good night – and dom you!' I asked a man one day, 'Do you know what o'clock it is?' he answered, 'Noa! and I don't want to.'

William Allingham (1868)

# April 11

I am perfectly well, and heed not the weather; though I wish the seasons came a little oftener into their own places instead of each Other's. From November, till a fortnight ago, we had much warmth that I should often be glad of in summer – and since we are not sure of it then, was rejoiced when I could get it.

Horace Walpole (1775)

# April 12

A fine, soft, showery morning saw us out of Boston, carrying with us the most pleasing reflections as to our reception and treatment there by numerous persons, none of whom we had ever seen before... At Sibsey, a pretty village five miles from Boston, we saw, for the first time since we left Peterborough, land rising above the level of the horizon; and, not having seen such a thing for so long, it had struck my daughters, who overtook me on the road (I having walked on from Boston), that the sight had an effect like that produced by the first sight of land after a voyage across the Atlantic.

William Cobbett (1830)

# April 13

Quite Summer-like Weather. Dinner a fine Pike boiled and Veal-Cutlets. Gave my Boy Billy Downing, he having been a very good lad and of most good natured turn and having asked Leave to go to Norwich with his Mother to Morrow-Morning to buy a Pair of Breeches &c. gave him this Even' 5.0.

James Woodforde (1792)

## April 14

Mr Ventris observed at Faringdon a little whirl-wind, which originated in the road before his house, taking up the dust & straws that came in its way. After mounting up thro' one of the elms before the Yard, & carrying away two of the rooks nests in which were young squabs; it then went off, leaving the court-yard strewed with dust & straws, & scraps of twigs, & the little naked rooks sprawling on the ground. A pair of rooks belonging to one of these nests built again, & had a late brood.

Gilbert White (1788)

## April 15

Quite a Summer's Day to-day. All Nature gay. Turnips quite a dead Load upon the Land. Many are obliged to throw them into Ditches &c. I am obliged to carry many off from Carys Close.

James Woodforde (1791)

Whan that Aprille with his shoures soote
The droghte of Marche hath perced to the roote,
And bathed every veyne in swich licour,
Of which vertu engendred is the flour;
Whan Zephirus eek with his sweete breeth
Inspired hath in every holt and heeth
The tendre croppes, and the yonge sonne
Hath in the Ram his halfe cours y-ronne,
And smale fowles maken melodye,
That slepen al the night with open ye,
(So priketh hem nature in hir corages);
Than longen folk to goon on pilgrimages,
And palmers for to seken straunge strondes,
To ferne halwes, couthe in sondry londes;
And specially, from every shires ende
Of Engelond, to Caunterbury they wende,
The holy blisful martir for to seke,
That hem hath holpen, whan that they were seke.

GEOFFREY CHAUCER, FROM THE PROLOGUE TO
*THE CANTERBURY TALES*

# April 16

Green wood-pecker laughs at all the world.
Storm-cock sings.

Gilbert White (1770)

# April 17

A journey in a railway train makes me sentimental. If I enter the compartment a robust-minded, cheerful youth, fresh and whistling from a walk by the sea, yet, as soon as I am settled down in one corner and the train is rattling along past fields, woods, towns, and painted stations, I find myself indulging in a saccharine sadness – very toothsome and jolly.

W. N. P. Barbellion (1911)

# April 18

Our weather is terribly rainy, though very fine between. We have got nightingales in the pleasure ground, and in the wood down near the sea. We are all extremely well, and expect the Prince of Prussia here to-day for two nights.

Queen Victoria (1848)

# April 19

Very thick Ice, & the Ground froze hard. Frequent showers of snow, & hail. The Hot-beds maintain their Heat well: the melon-beds too apt to steam; & the air too cold to be admitted in any great degree.

Gilbert White (1754)

# April 20

Soon after breakfast Mrs Davy of Foulsham with a Servant Boy with her on single Horses came to our House and she stayed and dined and spent the Afternoon with us, but went away before Tea back to Foulsham. We had for dinner a Fillet of Veal rosted and a nice boiled Ham, Tartletts &c. Mrs Davy was not well pleased with me nor I with her. She is without exception the most bold Woman I know.

James Woodforde (1789)

# April 21

Ah! I wish you were here to walk with me now that the warm weather is come at last. Things have been delayed but to be more welcome, and to burst forth twice as thick and beautiful. This is boasting however, and counting of the chickens before they are hatched: the East winds may again plunge us back into winter: but the sunshine of this morning fills one's pores with jollity, as if one had taken laughing gas.

Edward Fitzgerald (1837)

# April 22

A lovely summer morning which I spent in sauntering round the lawn at Monnington Rectory watching the waving of the birch tresses, listening to the sighing of the firs in the great solemn avenue, that vast Cathedral, and reading Robert Browning's 'In a Gondola' and thinking of dear Ettie... William and I walked up to the top of Moccas Park, whence we had a glorious view of the Golden Valley shining in the evening sunlight with the white houses of Dorstone scattered about the green hillsides 'like a handful of pearls in a cup of emerald' and the noble spire of Peterchurch rising from out of the heart of the beautiful rich valley which was closed below by the Sugar Loaf and the Skyrrid blue above Abergavenny.

Francis Kilvert (1876)

# April 23

From the inn at Spittal we came to this famous ancient Roman station, and afterwards grand scene of Saxon and Gothic splendour... It was the third or fourth day of the Spring fair, which is one of the greatest in the kingdom, and which lasts for a whole week. Horses begin the fair; then come sheep; and to-day, the horned-cattle. It is supposed that there were about 50,000 sheep, and I think the whole of the space in the various roads and streets, covered by the cattle, must have amounted to ten acres of ground or more.

William Cobbett (1830)

# April 24

A very wet day. William called me out to see a waterfall behind the barberry tree. We walked in the evening to Rydale. Coleridge and I lingered behind. C. stopped up the little runnel by the road-side to make a lake. We all stood to look at Glow-worm Rock – a primrose that grew there, and just looked out on the road from its own sheltered bower. The clouds moved, as William observed, in one regular body like a multitude of motion – a sky all clouds over, not one cloud. On our return it broke a little out, and we saw here and there a star. One appeared but for a moment in a pale blue sky.

Dorothy Wordsworth (1802)

# April 25

I think Edward will not suffer much longer from heat; by the look of things this morning I suspect the weather is rising into the balsamic north-east. It has been hot here, as you may suppose, since it was so hot with you, but I have not suffered from it at all, nor felt it in such a degree as to make me imagine it would be anything in the country.

Jane Austen (1811)

# April 26

Fine hot summer weather for these twelve days past, which has brought every thing on in a wonderful manner.

Gilbert White (1762)

# April 27

You say, 'You suppose my garden is to be Gothic too.' That can't be; Gothic is merely architecture; and as one has a satisfaction in imprinting the gloom of abbeys and cathedrals on one's house, so one's garden, on the contrary, is to be nothing but riot, and the gaiety of nature.

Horace Walpole (1753)

# April 28

I am glad you will relish June for Strawberry; by that time I hope the weather will have recovered its temper. At present it is horridly cross and uncomfortable; I fear we shall have a cold season; we cannot eat our summer and have our summer.

Horace Walpole (1761)

# April 29

Was that celebrated eclipse of the sun, so much threatened by the astrologers, and which had so exceedingly alarmed the whole nation that hardly any one would work, nor stir out of their houses. So ridiculously were they abused by knavish and ignorant star-gazers.

John Evelyn (1652)

# April 30

I never played golf. I do that sort of thing by deputy. K— is the sort of man to do it for me. At any rate, I trust him with my football and rowing. It doesn't tire you so much if you do it that way. Only let me give you one piece of advice, which I only wish I acted upon: 'Don't do your thinking by deputy': do your rowing, golf, football, cricket, skittles, talking if you like, but not your thinking.

Forbes Robinson (1892)

If ever I saw blessing in the air
I see it now in this still early day
Where lemon-green the vaporous morning drips
Wet sunlight on the powder of my eye.

Blown bubble-film of blue, the sky wraps round
Weeds of warm light whose every root and rod
Splutters with soapy green, and all the world
Sweats with the bead of summer in its bud.

If ever I heard blessing it is there
Where birds in trees that shoals and shadows are
Splash with their hidden wings and drops of sound
Break on my ears their crests of throbbing air.

Pure in the haze the emerald sun dilates,
The lips of sparrows milk the mossy stones,
While white as water by the lake a girl
Swims her green hand among the gathered swans.

Now, as the almond burns its smoking wick,
Dropping small flames to light the candled grass;
Now, as my low blood scales its second chance,
If ever world were blessed, now it is.

LAURIE LEE, 'APRIL RISE'

# *May*

Everything green and overflowing with life,
and the streams making a perpetual song,
with the thrushes, and all little birds...

Dorothy Wordsworth

Comes dancing from the East, and leads with her
The Flowry May, who from her green lap throws
The yellow Cowslip, and the pale Primrose.
Hail bounteous May that dost inspire
Mirth and youth, and warm desire,
Woods and Groves, are of thy dressing,
Hill and Dale, doth boast thy blessing.
Thus we salute thee with our early Song,
And welcome thee, and wish thee long.

JOHN MILTON, 'SONG ON MAY MORNING'

## May 1

This morning I was told how the people of Deal have set up two or three Maypoles, and have hung up their flags upon the top of them, and do resolve to be very merry to-day. It being a very pleasant day, I wished myself in Hyde Park.

Samuel Pepys (1660)

## May 2

The Hanger out in full leaf; but much banged about by the Continual strong East-wind that has blown for many days. The buds, & blossoms of all trees much injured by the wind. The ground parch'd, & bound very hard. The cold air keeps the nightingales very silent. No vegetation seems to stir at present.

Disbudded some of the vines: the buds are about an Inch long.

Gilbert White (1759)

# May 3

In one quarter was a May-pole dressed with garlands, and people dancing round it to a tabor and pipe and rustic music, all masqued, as were all the various bands of music that were disposed in different parts of the garden; some like huntsmen with French-horns, some like peasants, with a troop of harlequins and scaramouches in the little open temple on the mount. On the canal was a sort of gondola, adorned with flags and streamers, and filled with music, rowing about. All round the outside of the amphitheatre were shops, filled with Dresden china, Japan, etc. and all the shop-keepers in mask. The amphitheatre was illuminated; and in the middle was a circular bower, composed of all kinds of firs in tubs from twenty to thirty feet high: under them orange-trees, with small lamps in each orange, and below them all sorts of the finest auriculas in pots; and festoons of natural flowers hanging from tree to tree.

Horace Walpole (1749)

## May 4

To George Montagu, Esq.

Arlington Street, May 4, as they call it, but the weather and the almanack of my feelings affirm it is December.

Horace Walpole (1755)

## May 5

Our journey here was perfectly free from accident or event; we changed horses at the end of every stage, and paid at almost every turnpike. We had charming weather, hardly any dust, and were exceedingly agreeable, as we did not speak above once in three miles.

Jane Austen (1801)

# May 6

The small birds are singing, lambs bleating, cuckoos calling, the thrush sings by fits, Thomas Ashburner's axe is going quietly (without passion) in the orchard, hens are cackling, flies humming, the women talking together at their doors, plum and pear trees are in blossom – apple trees greenish – the opposite woods green, the crows are cawing, we have heard ravens, the ash trees are in blossom, birds flying all about us, the stitchwort is coming out, there is one budding lychnis, the primroses are passing their prime, celandine, violets, and wood sorrel for ever more, little geraniums and pansies on the wall.

Dorothy Wordsworth (1802)

## May 7

The weather is very fine and warm; the leaves of the Oaks are coming out very fast: some of the trees are nearly in half-leaf. The Birches are out in leaf. I do not think that I ever saw the wheat look, take it all together, so well as it does at this time. I see in the stiff land no signs of worm or slug. The winter, which destroyed so many turnips, must, at any rate, have destroyed these mischievous things. The oats look well. The barley is very young; but I do not see anything amiss with regard to it.

William Cobbett (1823)

# May 8

A strange tempestuous day, with violent thunder, storms of hail, & gluts of rain. Very cold weather before, & since.

Gilbert White (1763)

# May 9

Depressed tho' I was, I felt a great deliciousness in the quiet green lanes and hedges, thickets, woods and distances; and the evening after my arrival, standing at the field gate close to the Town, I heard four nightingales.

William Allingham (1863)

# May 10

I have a friend who to-day writes she is having iron rings driven into an old stone house round the windows so as to hold pots of Carnations and Geraniums, to hang down as they do in Tyrol and Switzerland. This will look pretty, no doubt, if it answers; but in our cold and windy summers I am sure they would do better if one pot were sunk inside another with some moss between, so that the evaporation caused by the wind, which freezes the roots, should not be so great.

Mrs C. W. Earle (1896)

# May 11

We breakfasted at Hungerford & at 10 we went on. My bay Mare coughed exceedingly between Hungerford & Farnborough worse than I ever knew her. I believe it to be owing to eating Beans only for Corn. At 4 this afternoon we set forth for Oxford and got there I thank God safe and well at about 9 o'clock we came on slow on Account of my Mare – I gave her no Beans at Farnborough only Oats well watered and she came on brave afterwards.

James Woodforde (1776)

# May 12

Fine rain after a long dry fit. Sowed a small crop of Roman-Broccoli.
Cucumbers in vast abundance, & very large.
The Succades offer fine fruit.

Gilbert White (1761)

# May 13

Oh, what a most delightful time it is, the birds tuning their melodious throats, and hymning their Creator's praise; whilst man, frail, degenerate man, lies supinely stretched on a bed of luxury and ease, or else is so immersed in the vain and empty pleasures of this world, that he is utterly forgetful of the goodness of the Supreme Being, that showers down His blessings upon him, and sheds plenteousness around his table!

Thomas Turner (1759)

# May 14

Having commenced gardener, I study the arts of pruning, sowing, and planting; and enterprise every thing in that way, from melons down to cabbages. I have a large garden to display my abilities in, and, were we twenty miles nearer London, I might turn higgler, and serve your honour with cauliflowers, and brocoli, at the best hand. I shall possibly now and then desire you to call at the seed-shop, in your way to Westminster, though sparingly. Should I do it often, you would begin to think you had a mother-in-law at Berkhampstead.

William Cowper (1767)

# May 15

We returned yesterday evening from Aldershot, where we spent two very pleasant days with very warm weather. Sunday was a beautiful day and we rode over to Farnham, the Bishop of Winchester's Palace, and it was quite beautiful, the country is so green and sweet – and enjoyable.

Queen Victoria (1860)

I cannot tell you how it was,
But this I know: it came to pass
Upon a bright and sunny day
When May was young; ah, pleasant May!
As yet the poppies were not born
Between the blades of tender corn;
The last egg had not hatched as yet,
Nor any bird foregone its mate.

I cannot tell you what it was,
But this I know: it did but pass.
It passed away with sunny May,
Like all sweet things it passed away,
And left me old, and cold, and gray.

CHRISTINA ROSSETTI, 'MAY'

# May 16

This afternoon I drove with my Father to Seagry through the snowy May bushes and golden brown oaks and lovely hedgerows of Sutton Lane. Charles Awdry went with us to the river and Seagry Mill, and we lay back on the river bank talking while my Father fished. It was a glorious afternoon, unclouded, and the meadows shone dazzling like a golden sea in the glory of the sheets of buttercups. The deep dark river, still and glassy, seemed to be asleep and motionless except when a leaf or blossom floated slowly by.

Francis Kilvert (1874)

# May 17

I went this morning upon a Hack to Wooton, where I read Prayers & Preached in the morning & read Prayers in ye Afternoon. Oglander Junr was to have went for Whitmore, but Oglander's Father being just now dead, he desired me to serve it. It rained all the way there, with the Wind directly in my Face.

James Woodforde (1767)

## May 18

Fierce storms of Hail, which batter'd the vine shoots at the end of the Dining-room very much. They were very forward this sunny spring: the leaves were cut full of Holes, & several shoots were beaten quite off the tress. The persicaria-plants in the border under suffered much.

Gilbert White (1760)

## May 19

Walked in the little garden, and saw the Falmouth plants which Clara cherishes so lovingly, and Henry's cactus and other dear memorials.

Caroline Fox (1840)

## May 20

A fine mild rain... Everything green and overflowing with life, and the streams making a perpetual song, with the thrushes, and all little birds, not getting the stone-chats. The post was not come in. I walked as far as Windermere, and met him there.

Dorothy Wordsworth (1800)

## May 21

So into my naked bed and slept till 9 o'clock, and then John Goods waked me, and by the captain's boy brought me four barrels of Mallows oysters, which Captain Tatnell had sent me from Murlace. The weather foul all this day also.

Samuel Pepys (1660)

## May 22

My first experience of the Moors came bursting in on me with a flood of ideas, impressions, and delights. I cannot write out the history of to-day. It would take too long and my mind is a palpitating tangle.

W. N. P. Barbellion (1907)

## May 23

How delightful to get down into the sweet fresh damp air of the country again and the scent of the bean blossoms.

Francis Kilvert (1873)

# May 24

You know my way of life so well that I need not describe it to you, as it has undergone no change since I saw you. I read of mornings; the same old books over and over again, having no command of new ones: walk with my great black dog of an afternoon, and at evening sit with open windows, up to which China roses climb, with my pipe, while the blackbirds and thrushes begin to rustle bedwards in the garden, and the nightingale to have the neighbourhood to herself. We have had such a spring (bating the last ten days) as would have satisfied even you with warmth. And such verdure! White clouds moving over the new fledged tops of oak trees, and acres of grass striving with buttercups.

Edward Fitzgerald (1844)

# May 25

We breakfasted, dined, supped & slept at Weston. My Servant Will dined, supped & slept at my House to Night. My Horses are at Leonade and to remain there till I can get some Hay and Straw for them. Mr Wilson Junr called upon me in the Afternoon. We were very dull again in the Evening being in a strange Place and things very inconvenient at present.

James Woodforde (1776)

# May 26

The weather for some days very sultry: to day was thunder &
rain; & in some places very heavy showers; but not at Selborne.

Gilbert White (1764)

# May 27

Sat upon a comfortable jetty of rock and watched the waves
without a glimmer of an idea in my mind about anything –
though to outward view I might have been a philosopher in
cerebral parturition with thoughts as big as babies.

W. N. P. Barbellion (1912)

# May 28

The season is wonderfully improved within this day or two;
and if these cloudless skies are continued to us, or rather if
the cold winds do not set in again, promises you a pleasant
excursion, as far, at least, as the weather can conduce to
make it such.

William Cowper (1781)

# May 29

Oak-apple day and the children all came to school with breast-knots of oak leaves.

Francis Kilvert (1876)

# May 30

Walking to Marnhull. The prime of bird-singing. The thrushes and blackbirds are the most prominent, – pleading earnestly rather than singing, and with such modulation that you seem to see their little tongues curl inside their bills in their emphasis. A bullfinch sings from a tree with a metallic sweetness piercing as a fife. Further on I come to a hideous carcase of a house in a green landscape, like a skull on a table of dessert.

Thomas Hardy (1877)

## May 31

You cannot imagine – it is not in human nature to imagine – what a nice walk we have round the orchard. The row of beech look very well indeed, and so does the young quickset hedge in the garden. I hear to-day that an apricot has been detected on one of the trees.

Jane Austen (1811)

Come we to the summer, to the summer we will come,
For the woods are full of bluebells and the hedges full of bloom,
And the crow is on the oak a-building of her nest,
And love is burning diamonds in my true lover's breast;
She sits beneath the whitethorn a-plaiting of her hair,
And I will to my true lover with a fond request repair;
I will look upon her face, I will in her beauty rest,
And lay my aching weariness upon her lovely breast.

The clock-a-clay is creeping on the open bloom of May,
The merry bee is trampling the pinky threads all day,
And the chaffinch it is brooding on its grey mossy nest
In the whitethorn bush where I will lean upon my lover's breast;
I'll lean upon her breast and I'll whisper in her ear
That I cannot get a wink o'sleep for thinking of my dear;
I hunger at my meat and I daily fade away
Like the hedge rose that is broken in the heat of the day.

JOHN CLARE, 'SUMMER'

# June

Another beautiful haymaking day. We all worked
hard and got the hay up in beautiful condition,
I pitching the last four loads with Jacob Knight.
We finished about nine o'clock of a lovely warm
Midsummer's Eve.

Francis Kilvert

Ask me no more where Jove bestows,
When June is past, the fading rose;
For in your beauty's orient deep
These flowers as in their causes, sleep.

Ask me no more whither doth stray
The golden atoms of the day;
For in pure love heaven did prepare
Those powders to enrich your hair.

Ask me no more whither doth haste
The nightingale when May is past;
For in your sweet dividing throat
She winters and keeps warm her note.

Ask me no more where those stars light
That downwards fall in dead of night;
For in your eyes they sit, and there,
Fixed become as in their sphere.

Ask me no more if east or west
The Phœnix builds her spicy nest;
For unto you at last she flies,
And in your fragrant bosom dies.

THOMAS CAREW, 'A SONG: WHEN JUNE
IS PAST, THE FADING ROSE'

# June 1

I sat up in the B.C.R. this Evening till after twelve o'clock, and then went to bed, and at three in the Morning, had my outward Doors broken open, my Glass Doors broke, and pulled out of Bed, and brought back into the B.C.R., where I was obliged to drink and smoak, but not without a good many Words. Peckham broke my doors, being very drunk, altho' they were open, which I do not relish of Mr Peckham much.

James Woodforde (1763)

# June 2

I certainly am glad of rain, but could wish it was boiled a little over the sun first: Mr Bentley calls this the hard summer, and says he is forced to buy his fine weather at Newcastle. Adieu!

Horace Walpole (1757)

# June 3

The season has been most unfavourable to animal life; and I, who am merely animal, have suffered much by it.

William Cowper (1783)

# June 4

Vehement hot dry weather for many days (a fortnight past) so that the fields & Gardens begin to suffer greatly. The early Cucumbers hardly bear at all tho' constantly water'd: & the melons swell very slowly.

Turn'd out the white Cucumbers from under the Glasses.

Gilbert White (1762)

# June 5

Lined-out the Cantaleupe-bed with twelve dung-carts of hot dung. The bed is now 12 feet broad, & 14 feet long. Continual showers all day: so that no loam could be laid on ye bed, but what was already housed in the earth-house. Fig-tree has plenty of fruit, which grows apace.

Such a violent Rain, & wind all the evening, & most part of the night that they broke-down & displaced the pease, & beans, & most of the flowers; & tore the hedges, & trees, & beat down several of the shrubs.

Gilbert White (1759)

# June 6

Out egg-collecting with the Lighthouse Keepers. They walk about the cliffs as surefooted as cats, and feed their dogs on birds' eggs collected in a little bag at the end of a long pole.

W. N. P. Barbellion (1909)

# June 7

Later the warm soft night was laden with perfume and the sweet scent of the syringa.

Francis Kilvert 1874

# June 8

Ellen and I rode to Windermere. We had a fine sunny day, neither hot nor cold. I mounted the horse at the quarry. We had no difficulties or delays but at the gates. I was enchanted with some of the views. From the High Ray the view is very delightful, rich, and festive, water and wood, houses, groves, hedgerows, green fields, and mountains; white houses, large and small. We passed two or three new-looking statesmen's houses. The Curwens' shrubberies looked pitiful enough under the native trees.

Dorothy Wordsworth (1802)

# June 9

During dinner hour, between morning and afternoon school, went out on the S— B— River Bank, and found another Sedge Warbler's nest. This is the fifth I have found this year. People who live opposite on the T— V— hear them sing at night and think they are Nightingales!

W. N. P. Barbellion (1905)

# June 10

Lord Melbourne earnestly hopes that your Majesty is well and not too much affected by the heat of this weather, which does not suit Lord Melbourne very well. In conjunction with a large dinner which we had at the Reform Club in honour of the Duke of Sussex, it has given Lord Melbourne a good deal of headache and indisposition. The Duke was in very good humour, and much pleased with the dinner, but he was by no means well or strong.

Viscount Melbourne (1842)

## June 11

It is exactly a month today since there has been any rain except a trifling shower or two that did not half lay ye dust. The fields & Gardens begin to suffer; & there is but a poor prospect of a Crop of hay; & most people's old stock is quite spent. There have been great showers about for this week past; but we have had none of them yet. The Succades have now many brace set; & there are a brace or two of Cantaleupes secure. The Succades have lost a fortnight for want of more water this severe dry season. Widen'd-out the Cantal: Bed before & behind, & laid-on a good depth of earth.

Gilbert White (1763)

# June 12

Bathing yesterday and to-day. Yesterday the sea was very calm, but the wind has changed to the East and this morning a rough and troublesome [sea] came tumbling into the bay and plunging in foam upon the shore. The bay was full of white horses. At Shanklin one has to adopt the detestable custom of bathing in drawers. If ladies don't like to see men naked why don't they keep away from the sight? To-day I had a pair of drawers given me which I could not keep on. The rough waves stripped them off and tore them down round my ancles. While thus fettered I was seized and flung down by a heavy sea which retreating suddenly left me lying naked on the sharp shingle from which I rose streaming with blood. After this I took the wretched and dangerous rag off and of course there were some ladies looking on as I came up out of the water.

Francis Kilvert (1874)

# June 13

This is a delightful day in the country, and I hope not much too hot for town. Well, you had a good journey, I trust, and all that, and not rain enough to spoil your bonnet. It appeared so likely to be a wet evening that I went up to the Gt House between three and four, and dawdled away an hour very comfortably, thought Edwd was not very brisk. The air was clearer in the evening and he was better. We all five walked together into the kitchen garden and along the Gosport road, and they drank tea with us.

Jane Austen (1814)

# June 14

Had a Bottle of Geree's Wine in the B.C.R. For Porter 0.0.2. For strong Beer at a Place in Holliwell, with Hearst, Loggin, Bell, Russell, & Ballard where we spent the Evening, and I paid there 0.1.0. Hearst, Bell & myself, being in Beer, went under Whitmore's Window, and abused him very much, as being dean, he came down, and sent us to our Proper Rooms, and then we Huzza'd him again, & again. We are to wait on him to Morrow.

James Woodforde (1761)

## I

June was not over
Though past the fall,
And the best of her roses
Had yet to blow,
When a man I know
(But shall not discover,
Since ears are dull,
And time discloses)
Turned him and said with a man's true air,
Half sighing a smile in a yawn, as 'twere, –
'If I tire of your June, will she greatly care?'

## II

Well, dear, in-doors with you!
True! serene deadness
Tries a man's temper.
What's in the blossom
June wears on her bosom?
Can it clear scores with you?
Sweetness and redness.
– *Eadem semper!* –
Go, let me care for it greatly or slightly!
If June mend her bower now, your hand left unsightly
By plucking the roses, – my June will do rightly.

### III

And after, for pastime,
If June be refulgent
With flowers in completeness,
All petals, no prickles,
Delicious as trickles
Of wine poured at mass-time, –
And choose One indulgent
To redness and sweetness:
Or if, with experience of man and of spider,
June use my June-lightning, the strong insect-ridder,
And stop the fresh film-work, – why, June will consider.

ROBERT BROWNING, 'ANOTHER WAY OF LOVE'

# June 15

Dr Calvert joined us at dinner, and we all lounged under our drooping spruce, with Balaam the ape, which I had borrowed for the afternoon, in the foreground, and the kid near by, quite happy in our companionship.

Caroline Fox (1841)

# June 16

I hope you have had as favourable Succession of sun and rain as we have.

Horace Walpole (1758)

# June 17

At eleven, at this season (and how much longer I know not), there is still a twilight. If we could only have such dry, deliciously warm evenings as we used to have in our own land, what enjoyment there might be in these interminable twilights! But here we close the window-shutters, and make ourselves cosey by a coal-fire.

All three of the children, and, I think, my wife and myself, are going through the hooping-cough. The east-wind of this season and region is most horrible. There have been no really warm days; for though the sunshine is sometimes hot, there is never any diffused heat throughout the air. On passing from the sunshine into the shade, we immediately feel too cool.

Nathaniel Hawthorne (1854)

# June 18

Mowed the greatest part of the great mead: but was deterr'd from finishing the whole by a vast tempest of thunder & lightening that lay along to the N: W; N: & E: all the afternoon. It thundered loudly for hours together; but not one drop fell with us. The heat, being reflected from white thunder-clouds, was unusually severe.

The weather cock stood all day plumb S: but the storm came-up from the N: W: There is a very fine crop of Grass in the meadow. This day has burnt & scalded things in the Gardens in a strange manner. Gave the Cantaleupes a good watering within the frames: but gave no water to the Succades, as many brace of them, at least ten, are full grown, & near ripening.

Gilbert White (1764)

# June 19

From Kensington to this place, through Edgware, Stanmore, and Watford, the crop is almost entirely hay, from fields of permanent grass, manured by dung and other matter brought from the Wen. Near the Wen, where they have had the first haul of the Irish and other perambulating labourers, the hay is all in rick. Some miles further down it is nearly all in. Towards Stanmore and Watford, a third, perhaps, of the grass remains to be cut. It is curious to see how the thing regulates itself.

William Cobbett (1822)

# June 20

Thankes-giving-day for victory over ye Dutch... Thence after dinner, to White Hall with Sir W. Berkely in his coach, and so walked to Herbert's and there spent a little time... Thence by water to Fox-hall, and there walked an hour alone, observing the several humours of the citizens that were there this holyday, pulling of cherries, – [The game of bob-cherry] – and God knows what, and so home to my office, where late, my wife not being come home with my mother, who have been this day all abroad upon the water, my mother being to go out of town speedily. So I home and to supper and to bed, my wife come home when I come from the office.

Samuel Pepys (1665)

The bonny month of June is crowned
With the sweet scarlet rose;
The groves and meadows all around
With lovely pleasure flows.

As I walked out to yonder green,
One evening so fair;
All where the fair maids may be seen
Playing at the bonfire.

Hail! lovely nymphs, be not too coy,
But freely yield your charms;
Let love inspire with mirth and joy,
In Cupid's lovely arms.

Bright Luna spreads its light around,
The gallants for to cheer;
As they lay sporting on the ground,
At the fair June bonfire.

All on the pleasant dewy mead,
They shared each other's charms;
Till Phoebus' beams began to spread,
And coming day alarms.

Whilst larks and linnets sing so sweet,
To cheer each lovely swain;
Let each prove true unto their love,
And so farewell the plain.

CORNISH MIDSUMMER BONFIRE SONG

## *Midsummer's Eve*

*Another beautiful haymaking day. We all worked hard and got the hay up in beautiful condition, I pitching the last four loads with Jacob Knight. We finished about nine o'clock of a lovely warm Midsummer's Eve.*

Francis Kilvert (1875)

## June 21

Near the keeper's cottage the setting sun made a green and golden splendour in the little open glade among the oaks while the keeper and two other men walked like three angels in the gilded mist.

Francis Kilvert (1873)

# June 22

Thunder in the morning; & a little shattering of rain, being the skirts of the storm: clear burning weather the rest of the day.

Gilbert White (1764)

# June 23

One Prince a Shoemaker at Bruton came here this Afternoon to measure me for a Pair of Shoes for which I am to pay him when he brings them home 0.5.0. This Prince being a musical Man, I desired him to tune my Spinnett for me, which he did and pretty well, but would have nothing for it. N.B. My chief Intent for sending for him was to tune my Spinnett for I have at present Shoes sufficient.

James Woodforde (1764)

# June 24

Heard Spurgeon preach in a tent in a field beside the town. 'If any man thirst etc', anecdotes – prayer – good lungs. Rain – Spurgeon put on his hat, many opened umbrellas.

William Allingham (1863)

## June 25

The annuals are sadly scorch'd by the heat. The Succades, considering the long shady season they grew-in, & the early season if ripening, are good, & well-flavoured.

Put-up two loads of clover-hay on the rick, & covered it well with straw.

Gilbert White (1761)

## June 26

The country about, though not romantic or picturesque, is very pleasing; the surface slowly varied; and we have plenty of wood, but a sad want of water...

Dorothy Wordsworth (1791)

## June 27

Walked to V—. As usual, Nature with clockwork regularity had all her taps turned on – larks singing, cherries ripening, and bees humming.

W. N. P. Barbellion (1909)

# June 28

In the even, Joseph Fuller and myself plaid a game of cricket with Mr Geo. Banister and James Fuller, for half a crown's worth of punch, which we won very easy, but it being hot and drinking a pretty deal of punch, it got into my head, so that I came home not sober.

Thomas Turner (1763)

# June 29

Just as all the grass was spread-about came a great rain all day from the east: the only rain to do any good for six weeks, & three days.

Gilbert White (1763)

# June 30

Not but that the garden choir sang shrill, and two or three cocks, taunting, far away, lifted up their voices on stilts out of the dawning, crying, 'Cock-a-doodle-doo!'

James Smetham (1877)

Yes. I remember Adlestrop –
The name, because one afternoon
Of heat the express-train drew up there
Unwontedly.  It was late June.

The steam hissed.  Someone cleared his throat.
No one left and no one came
On the bare platform. What I saw
Was Adlestrop – only the name.

And willows, willow-herb, and grass,
And meadowsweet, and haycocks dry,
No whit less still and lonely fair
Than the high cloudlets in the sky.

And for that minute a blackbird sang
Close by, and round him, mistier,
Farther and farther, all the birds
Of Oxfordshire and Gloucestershire.

EDWARD THOMAS, 'ADLESTROP'

# July

A long beautiful road, dark, green and cool and
completely overarched with trees, led towards the sea
and in a high meadow the haymakers in their white
shirt sleeves, the dark horses and the high loaded
wagon stood out clear against the brilliant blue
waters of the Channel.

Francis Kilvert

Blue July, bright July,
Month of storms and gorgeous blue;
Violet lightnings o'er thy sky,
Heavy falls of drenching dew;
Summer crown! o'er glen and glade
Shrinking hyacinths in their shade;
I welcome thee with all thy pride,
I love thee like an Eastern bride.
Though all the singing days are done
As in those climes that clasp the sun;
Though the cuckoo in his throat
Leaves to the dove his last twin note;
Come to me with thy lustrous eye,
Golden-dawning oriently,
Come with all thy shining blooms,
Thy rich red rose and rolling glooms.
Though the cuckoo doth but sing 'cuk, cuk,'
And the dove alone doth coo;
Though the cushat spins her coo-r-roo, r-r-roo –
To the cuckoo's halting 'cuk.'

GEORGE MEREDITH, FROM 'JULY'

# July 1

Up betimes, about 9 o'clock, waked by a damned noise between a sow gelder and a cow and a dog, nobody after we were up being able to tell us what it was. After being ready we took coach, and, being very sleepy, droused most part of the way to Gravesend, and there 'light, and down to the new batterys, which are like to be very fine, and there did hear a plain fellow cry out upon the folly of the King's officers above... Then informed ourselves where we might have some creame, and they guided us to one Goody Best's, a little out of the towne towards London road, and thither we went with the coach, and find it a mighty clean, plain house, and had a dish of very good creame to our liking, and so away presently very merry, and fell to reading of the several Advices to a Painter, which made us good sport, and indeed are very witty...

Samuel Pepys (1667)

# July 2

I am looking out upon a dark gray sea, with a keen north-east wind blowing it in shore. It is more like late autumn than midsummer, and there is a howling in the air as if the latter were in a very hopeless state indeed. The very Banshee of Midsummer is rattling the windows drearily while I write.

Charles Dickens (1847)

# July 3

It is so settled that we are never to have tolerable weather in June, that the first hot day was on Saturday-hot by comparison: for I think it is three years since we have really felt the feel of summer. I was, however, concerned to be forced to come to town yesterday on some business; for, however the country feels, it looks divine, and the verdure we buy so dear is delicious.

Horace Walpole (1769)

# July 4

All our family, except my mother, are collected here: all my brothers and sisters, with their wives, husbands, and children: sitting at different occupations, or wandering about the grounds and gardens, discoursing each their separate concerns, but all united into one whole. The weather is delightful: and when I see them passing to and fro, and hear their voices, it is like scenes of a play. I came here only yesterday. I have much to tell you of: I mean, much in my small way: I will keep all till I see you, for I don't know with what to begin in a letter.

Edward Fitzgerald (1835)

# July 5

This morning my brother Tom brought me my jackanapes coat with silver buttons. It rained this morning, which makes us fear that the glory of this great day will be lost; the King and Parliament being to be entertained by the City to-day with great pomp.

Samuel Pepys (1660)

# July 6

Mr Cecil, the other day, was saying that England could produce as fine peaches as any other country. I asked what was the particular excellence of a peach, and he answered, 'Its cooling and refreshing quality, like that of a melon!' Just think of this idea of the richest, most luscious, of all fruits! But the untravelled Englishman has no more idea of what fruit is than of what sunshine is; he thinks he has tasted the first and felt the last, but they are both alike watery. I heard a lady in Lord Street talking about the 'broiling sun,' when I was almost in a shiver. They keep up their animal heat by means of wine and ale, else they could not bear this climate.

Nathaniel Hawthorne (1854)

# July 7

Finished my Hay-rick in most excellent order. The weather has been so perfectly hot, & bright for these five days past that my Hay was all cut, & made in that time. The Crop was so great that Kelsey's people made 8 carryings of it: & the burden in the great mead was supposed to be considerably greater than ever was known. To my own stock I added two tons from Farmer Lassam, which in all make a considerable rick.

Finished cutting the hedges round Baker's Hill.

Gilbert White (1759)

# July 8

I consider no trouble too great, whether the garden be large or small, to grow the beautiful stately Madonna Lily (*Lilium candidum*).

Mrs C. W. Earle (1896)

## July 9

I breakfasted, supped & slept again at Ansford. I went a fishing by myself this morning down to Week Bridge and angled from there to Cole, and there I dined & spent the Afternoon at Mr Guppeys with him his Sister and Mr Pounsett. We had for Dinner some bacon & beans, a Shoulder of Mutton & Currant Pye. I caught 3 Trout, the largest being 14 Inches & half long Which I caught with 2 Grasshoppers & a small hook.

James Woodforde (1779)

# July 10

This is about the time we move our things from the reserve garden, spoken of before, and from the late-sown seed beds, and plant into the borders and square beds those amiable autumn annuals that do not seem to mind moving at all, such as French Marigolds, Tagetes, Everlastings, Scabious, &c.

Mrs C. W. Earle (1896)

# July 11

Came at length to Bury, only four miles from Arundel; but our horse wanted rest after so toilsome a road, and we drank tea, before beginning to mount one of the prodigious hills we had long seen. Came at last to the fine downs on its summit, whence a world seemed to lie before us.

Ann Ward Radcliffe (1800)

## July 12

A little above Dacre we came into the right road to Mr Clarkson's, after having walked through woods and fields, never exactly knowing whether we were right or wrong. We learnt, however, that we had saved half-a-mile. We sate down by the river-side to rest, and saw some swallows flying about and under the bridge, and two little schoolboys were loitering among the scars seeking after their nests.

Dorothy Wordsworth (1802)

## July 13

The morning was blue and lovely with a warm sun and fresh breeze blowing from the sea and the Culver Downs... Bosomed amongst green, pretty cottages peeped through the thick foliage and here and there a garden shone brilliant with flowers. A long beautiful road, dark, green and cool and completely overarched with trees, led towards the sea and in a high meadow the haymakers in their white shirt sleeves, the dark horses and the high loaded wagon stood out clear against the brilliant blue waters of the Channel.

Francis Kilvert (1875)

# July 14

We are very happily established here since Thursday, and have beautiful weather for this truly enjoyable place; we drive, walk, and sit out – and the nights are so fine.

Queen Victoria (1846)

# July 15

Oh, how useful and beautiful are the tall yellow and the tall white Snapdragons! They can be played with in so many ways: potted up in the autumn, grown and flowered in a greenhouse, cut back and planted out in the spring to flower again, admirable to send away; in fact, they have endless merits, and in a large clump in front of some dark corner or shrub they look very handsome indeed. They are lovely picked and on the dinner-table, especially the yellow Snapdragons, but, like many other things, they just want a little care and cultivation, which they often do not get; and they ought to be sown every April, and again in July.

Mrs C. W. Earle (1896)

# July 16

This morning it proved very rainy weather so that I could not remove my goods to my house. I to my office and did business there, and so home, it being then sunrise, but by the time that I got to my house it began to rain again, so that I could not carry my goods by cart as I would have done. After that to my Lord's and so home and to bed.

Samuel Pepys (1660)

# July 17

We see the Fleet at Spithead, 'like Milan Cathedral.' Rain comes on. The Queen having reached the French Fleet – Ironclads, huge, black and ugly, – royal salutes thunder, the yards are manned, but we can see very little for the thick weather. Ryde Pier, Tennyson and I land, among others; the ladies ill and draggled. Pier Hotel. A. T., Charles T., and I go up High Street and out into a field beyond, where we sit on a balk of wood, looking at some cows grazing, and A. T. smoking.

William Allingham (1867)

# July 18

Thence to my Lord about business, and being in talk in comes one with half a buck from Hinchinbroke, and it smelling a little strong my Lord did give it me (though it was as good as any could be). I did carry it to my mother, where I had not been a great while, and indeed had no great mind to go, because my father did lay upon me continually to do him a kindness at the Wardrobe, which I could not do because of my own business being so fresh with my Lord. But my father was not at home, and so I did leave the venison with her to dispose of as she pleased. After that home, where W. Hewer now was, and did lie this night with us, the first night. My mind very quiet, only a little trouble I have for the great debts which I have still upon me to the Secretary, Mr Kipps, and Mr Spong for my patent.

Samuel Pepys (1660)

# July 19

Went to see the rural village of Alfriston, over such a road as I never saw before; and leading over such hills! Two men helped the chaise down one of them. Some finely spreading oaks about the village, which stands on an eminence in a green valley backed by grey downs.

Ann Ward Radcliffe (1800)

On these white cliffs, that calm above the flood
Uplift their shadowing heads, and, at their feet,
Scarce hear the surge that has for ages beat,
Sure many a lonely wanderer has stood;
And whilst the lifted murmur met his ear,
And o'er the distant billows the still eve
Sailed slow, has thought of all his heart must leave
Tomorrow; of the friends he loved most dear;
Of social scenes, from which he wept to part;
But if, like me, he knew how fruitless all
The thoughts that would full fain the past recall,
Soon would he quell the risings of his heart,
And brave the wild winds and unhearing tide,
The world his country, and his God his guide.

WILLIAM LISLE BOWLES, 'SONNET: AT DOVER CLIFFS'

# July 20

The weather has been most glorious, and the country, of course, most delightful. Our own valley in particular was last night, by the light of the full moon, and in the perfect stillness of the lake, a scene of loveliness and repose as affecting as was ever beheld by the eye of man.

William Wordsworth (1804)

# July 21

A splendid summer's day, burning hot, sitting under the linden reading *Memorials of a Quiet Life*, Augustus Hare's book. As I sat there my mind went through a fierce struggle. Right or wrong? The right conquered, the sun was repented and put away and the rustle of the wind and the melodious murmurs of innumerable bees in the hives overhead suddenly seemed to me to take the sound of distant music, organs.

Francis Kilvert (1873)

# July 22

The Hertfords carried me to dine at Lord Archer's, an odious place. On my return, I saw Warwick, a pretty old town, small, and thinly inhabited, in the form of a cross. The castle is enchanting; the view pleased me more than I can express; the river Avon tumbles down a cascade at the foot of it. It is well laid out by one Brown who has set up on a few ideas of Kent and Mr Southcote. One sees what the prevalence of taste does; little Brooke, who would have chuckled to have been born in an age of clipt hedges and cockle-shell avenues, has submitted to let his garden and park be natural.

Horace Walpole (1751)

# July 23

Mrs De Quetteville pointed out to Teddy with great pride the pond of delicious water which supplied the house with drinking water. At that moment, as she was assuring him that the water was perfectly pure, a large evet rose to the surface and stared at them while water spiders and amphidious beetles rowed about the pond.

Francis Kilvert (1872)

# July 24

Here I am again in the land of old Bunyan – better still in the land of the more perennial Ouse, making many a fantastic winding and going much out of his direct way to fertilize and adorn. Fuller supposes that he lingers thus in the pleasant fields of Bedfordshire, being in no hurry to enter the more barren fens of Lincolnshire. So he says. This house is just on the edge of the town: a garden on one side skirted by the public road which again is skirted by a row of such Poplars as only the Ouse knows how to rear – and pleasantly they rustle now – and the room in which I write is quite cool and opens into a greenhouse which opens into said garden: and it's all deuced pleasant.

Edward Fitzgerald (1839)

# July 25

One of the most beautiful of late summer plants – I see my friends often fail with it – is the *Lobelia cardinalis* and *L. fulgens*, Queen Victoria. It is generally injured by kindness, sown in the early spring, drawn up in greenhouses, and planted out weak and straggling, when it does nothing.

Mrs C. W. Earle (1896)

# July 26

Came from the Wen, through Croydon. It rained nearly all the way. The corn is good. A great deal of straw. The barley very fine; but all are backward; and if this weather continue much longer, there must be that 'heavenly blight' for which the wise friends of 'social order' are so fervently praying. But if the wet now cease, or cease soon, what is to become of the 'poor souls of farmers' God only knows!

William Cobbett (1823)

# July 27

All plants that have been planted out, after being removed from a reserve garden or seed bed, must be watered; and once you begin, whether in kitchen or flower garden, you must go on till it rains steadily and well; a slight shower is no good.

Mrs C. W. Earle (1896)

# July 28

This morning Teddy set up the net and poles in the field just opposite the dining room windows and we began to play 'sphairistrike' or lawn tennis, a capital game, but rather too hot for a summer's day.

Francis Kilvert (1874)

# July 29

A vast rain. The hay lies about in a miserable way.

Gilbert White (1763)

# July 30

I wish you could see him in his best *pose*, – when I have
arrested him in a violent career of carpet-scratching, and he
looks at me with fore-legs very wide apart, trying to penetrate
the deep mystery of this arbitrary, not to say capricious,
prohibition. He is snoring by my side at this moment, with
a serene promise of remaining quiet for any length of time:
he could behave better if he had been expressly educated
for me. I am too lazy a lover of dogs and all earthly things
to like them when they give me much trouble, preferring to
describe the pleasure other people have in taking trouble.

George Eliot (1859)

# July 31

We mounted the Dover Coach at Charring Cross. It was a
beautiful morning. The city, St Paul's, with the river and a
multitude of little boats, made a most beautiful sight as we
crossed Westminster Bridge.

Dorothy Wordsworth (1802)

What ails my senses thus to cheat?
What is it ails the place,
That all the people in the street
Should wear one woman's face?

The London trees are dusty-brown
Beneath the summer sky;
My love, she dwells in London town,
Nor leaves it in July.

O various and intricate maze,
Wide waste of square and street;
Where, missing through unnumbered days,
We twain at last may meet!

And who cries out on crowd and mart?
Who prates of stream and sea?
The summer in the city's heart –
That is enough for me.

AMY LEVY, 'LONDON IN JULY'

# August

We lack not songs, nor instruments of joy,
Nor echoes sweet, nor waters clear as heaven,
Nor laurel wreaths against the sultry heat.

WILLIAM BLAKE

## I

A shaded lamp and a waving blind,
And the beat of a clock from a distant floor:
On this scene enter – winged, horned, and spined –
A longlegs, a moth, and a dumbledore;
While 'mid my page there idly stands
A sleepy fly, that rubs its hands . . .

## II

Thus meet we five, in this still place,
At this point of time, at this point in space.
– My guests parade my new-penned ink,
Or bang at the lamp-glass, whirl, and sink.
'God's humblest, they!' I muse. Yet why?
They know Earth-secrets that know not I.

THOMAS HARDY, 'AN AUGUST MIDNIGHT'

# August 1

Cut the first melon. Mem: It hung too long & was mealy. This was intended for a Cantaleupe, but proved a common sort.

Gilbert White (1755)

# August 2

Ever since the middle of March I have been trying remedies for the *hooping-cough*, and have, I believe, tried everything, except riding, wet to the skin, two or three hours amongst the clouds on the South Downs. This remedy is now under trial.

William Cobbett (1823)

# August 3

I thank God, had a tolerable good Night last Night. Drank very little Wine yesterday or to day only 2 or 3 Glasses. I used myself before and all last Winter to near a Pint of Port Wine every Day and I now believe did me much harm.

James Woodforde (1790)

# August 4

Since I have been in Liverpool we have hardly had a day, until yesterday, without more or less of rain, and so cold and shivery that life was miserable. I am not warm enough even now, but am gradually getting acclimated in that respect.

Nathaniel Hawthorne (1853)

# August 5

Battel Abbey stands at the end of the town, exactly as Warwick Castle does of Warwick; but the house of Webster have taken due care that it should not resemble it in any thing else. A vast building, which they call the old refectory, but which I believe was the original church, is now barn, coach-house, etc. The situation is noble, above the level of abbeys: what does remain of gateways and towers is beautiful, particularly the flat side of a cloister, which is now the front of the mansion-house. Miss of the family has clothed a fragment of a portico with cockle-shells!

Horace Walpole (1752)

# August 6

I hope you did not suffer so severely as we did from the arctic cold that rushed in after the oppressive heat. Mr T. Trollope came from Italy just when it began. He says it is always the same when he comes to England, – people always say it has just been very hot, and he believes that means they had a few days in which they were not obliged to blow on their fingers.

George Eliot (1865)

# August 7

Tunbridge, Friday.
We are returned hither, where we have established our head-quarters. On our way, we had an opportunity of surveying that formidable mountain, Silver Hill, which we had floundered down in the dark: it commands a whole horizon of the richest blue prospect you ever saw.

Horace Walpole (1752)

# August 8

Trimmed the vines for the last time, & took-off their side-shoots.

The grapes swell & are very forward.

The pair of martins which build by the stair-case window, where their first brood came-out on July 7: are now hatching a second brood, as appears by some egg-shells thrown-out.

Gilbert White (1778)

# August 9

Bill behaved very saucy again this morning at breakfast and it made me very unhappy. It will not do at all.

James Woodforde (1778)

# August 10

As we journeyed along the fair Sussex shore between the plain and the sea the gleaners were busy in the golden stubbles, the windmills whirled their arms in the fresh sea breeze, the shocks of corn circling changed places swiftly like a dance of fairies, and Chichester steeple rose fair and white far over the meads.

Francis Kilvert (1874)

## August 11

Very hot, so went to S—, and bathed in the salmon pool. Stretched myself out in the water, delighted to find that I had at last got to the very heart of the countryside. I was not just watching from the outside – on the bank. I was in it, and plunging in it, too, up to my armpits.

W. N. P. Barbellion (1911)

## August 12

In the night there was a torrent of rain but the morning broke clear and beautiful. I went out early into the town before breakfast and walked along the beach. Sea and town and everything were sparkling bright and clean after the storm in the clear shining after the rain.

Francis Kilvert (1874)

# August 13

Frequent heavy thundershowers with hot growing weather.

Gilbert White (1762)

# August 14

We are still here; profiting by the bad sea, to visit many beautiful points de vue in this really beautiful country. We saw yesterday one of the loveliest places possible –Endsleigh – the Duke of Bedford's, about twenty miles from here.

The weather is so bad, and it blows so hard, that we shall go back to Southampton to-morrow by railroad – a beautiful line which we have never seen. I must close in haste.

Queen Victoria (1856)

# August 15

A hot, sultry afternoon, during most of which I was stretched out on the grass beside an upturned stone where a battle royal was fought between Yellow and Black Ants. The victory went to the hardy little Yellows... By the way, I held a Newt by the tail to-day and it emitted a squeak! So that the Newt has a voice after all.

W. N. P. Barbellion (1905)

O thou who passest thro' our valleys in
Thy strength, curb thy fierce steeds, allay the heat
That flames from their large nostrils! thou, O
Summer,
Oft pitched'st here thy golden tent, and oft
Beneath our oaks hast slept, while we beheld
With joy thy ruddy limbs and flourishing hair.

Beneath our thickest shades we oft have heard
Thy voice, when noon upon his fervid car
Rode o'er the deep of heaven; beside our springs
Sit down, and in our mossy valleys, on
Some bank beside a river clear, throw thy
Silk draperies off, and rush into the stream:
Our valleys love the Summer in his pride.

Our bards are fam'd who strike the silver wire:
Our youth are bolder than the southern swains:
Our maidens fairer in the sprightly dance:
We lack not songs, nor instruments of joy,
Nor echoes sweet, nor waters clear as heaven,
Nor laurel wreaths against the sultry heat.

WILLIAM BLAKE, 'TO SUMMER'

# August 16

I might date my letter from the green-house, which we have converted into a summer parlour. The walls hung with garden mats, and the floor covered with a carpet, the sun too in a great measure excluded, by an awning of mats which forbids him to shine any where except upon the carpet, it affords us by far the pleasantest retreat in Olney.

William Cowper (1781)

# August 17

A pretty fine day with a brisk drying wind. Many people were housing wheat all day, which went-in in better condition that could be expected.

Gilbert White (1764)

# August 18

We came to Hampstead Heath, and looked past a foreground of fir-trees over a wide undulating prospect tufted with trees, and richly cultivated, a lake shining in the distance under the evening sky. On the other side huge London lying sombre and silent.

William Allingham (1849)

# August 19

After dinner a thunderstorm with rain. Night grows pitch dark. Tremendous thunder and lightning for a long time. I put out my candle and sit at window watching. The lightning over the Island. A thunder-bolt apparently falls on the mainland eastwards. 'Tremble. Thou wretch.'

William Allingham (1867)

# August 20

This being Saturday, there early commenced a throng of visitants to Rock Ferry. The boat in which I came over brought from the city a multitude of factory-people. They had bands of music, and banners inscribed with the names of the mills they belong to, and other devices: pale-looking people, but not looking exactly as if they were underfed.

Nathaniel Hawthorne (1853)

# August 21

I stayed and dined at Ham, and after dinner Lady Dysart, with Lady Bridget Tollemache took our four nieces on the water to see the return of the barges but were to set me down at Lady Browne's. We were, with a footman and the two watermen, ten in a little boat. As we were in the middle of the river, a larger boat full of people drove directly upon us on purpose. I believe they were drunk. We called to them, to no purpose; they beat directly against the middle of our little skiff – but, thank you, did not do us the least harm – no thanks to them.

Horace Walpole (1778)

# August 22

Cut the first Cantaleupe, a very small one it was almost cleft in two: was high-flavour'd, & vastly superior to any of the Romanias. This Melon set the first of any; & was full 8 weeks in ripening. The plant on which this grew was one of the first crop, the only one that survived; & was moved in a careless manner back into the seedling-bed; & brought back again when the bed was new-worked-up.

Constant heavy rains for a week: the wheat that is down begins to grow.

Gilbert White (1756)

# August 23

About four P.M., I walked down to Halland, with several more of my neighbours, in order for a rejoicing for the taking of Cape Breton, &c., where there was a bonfire of six hundred of faggots, the cannon fired, and two barrels of beer given to the populace, and a very good supper provided for the principal tradesmen of this and the neighbouring parishes, as there had been a dinner for the gentlemen of Lewes and the neighbouring parishes.

Thomas Turner (1758)

# August 24

Sunday evening, walked to Latterrigg with Sara and Hartley – the sun set with slant columns of misty light, slanted from him: the light a bright buff – Walla Crag purple red, the lake Derwentwater a deep dingy purple blue – that Torrent Crag... a maroon. But the clouds... a fine *smoke-flame*... As we turned round on our return, we see a moving pillar of clouds, flame and smoke, rising, bending, arching, and in swift motion – from what God's chimney doth it issue?

Samuel Taylor Coleridge (1800)

## August 25

I went to Britford Vicarage to stay with the Morrises till Saturday. Late in the evening we loitered down into the water meads. The sun was setting in stormy splendour behind Salisbury and the marvellous aerial spire rose against the yellow glare like Ithuriel's spear, while the last gleams of the sunset flamed down the long lines of the water carriages making them shine and glow like canals of molten gold.

Francis Kilvert (1875)

## August 26

If you love good roads, conveniences, good inns, plenty of postilions and horses, be so kind as never to go into Sussex. We thought ourselves in the northest part of England; the whole country has a Saxon air, and the inhabitants are savage, as if King George the Second had been the first monarch of the East Angles. Coaches grow there no more than balm and spices; we were forced to drop our postchaise, that resembled nothing so much as harlequin's calash, which was occasionally a chaise or a baker's cart. We journeyed over Alpine mountains, drenched in clouds, and thought of harlequin again, when he was driving the chariot of the sun through the morning clouds, and so was glad to hear the aqua vitae man crying a dram.

Horace Walpole (1749)

# August 27

To Aldworth. Tennyson on lawn with Dr Grailey Hewitt, who has taken a house down here.

Ghosts – T. said, 'My grandfather, one night sitting up late reading, at College, looked up and saw, close to him, the ugliest old woman he ever saw in his life; and he also saw his cap and gown, which were hanging on the wall, going round and round the room. He shut up his book and said, "I'd better not read any more for the present."'

Tennyson looked very fine to-day, grandly simple, gently dignified: the marks round his mouth soft in expression as dimples.

William Allingham (1886)

# August 28

The continual sunny weather had brought on the Cantaleupes before I expected them, & madde them come almost all in a week. They were divided among our Neighbours, & were much commended.

I found the annuals very handsome & very strong; the Savoys strangely grown; & the Endives very large. Tull had planted out rows of Sweet-Williams, & Stocks in my absence.

Gilbert White (1761)

# August 29

Yesterday we all took a walk into the country. It was a fine afternoon, with clouds, of course, in different parts of the sky, but a clear atmosphere, bright sunshine, and altogether a Septembrish feeling. The ramble was very pleasant, along the hedge-lined roads in which there were flowers blooming, and the varnished holly, certainly one of the most beautiful shrubs in the world, so far as foliage goes.

Nathaniel Hawthorne (1853)

# August 30

We have walked to Rowling on each of the two last days after dinner, and very great was my pleasure in going over the house and grounds. We have also found time to visit all the principal walks of this place, except the walk round the top of the park, which we shall accomplish probably to-day.

Jane Austen (1805)

# August 31

When I went out with Jock this morning to walk across the common before breakfast there as usual were the three white tiddling lambs lying around the white gate. Immediately the three bold white lambs began to play with the black dog, to hunt him about and butt him sportively, while the dog with his ears laid back pretended to be afraid of the lambs, ran away from them, bounded back, faced them and occasionally took one of them by the ear.

I love to wander on these soft gentle and mournful autumn days, alone among the quiet peaceful solitary meadows, tracing out the ancient footpaths and mossy overgrown stiles between farm and hamlet, village and town, musing of the many feet that have trodden these ancient and now well nigh deserted and almost forgotten ways and walking in the footsteps of the generations that have gone before and passed away.

Francis Kilvert (1874)

The wind has swept from the wide atmosphere
Each vapour that obscured the sunset's ray,
And pallid Evening twines its beaming hair
In duskier braids around the languid eyes of Day:
Silence and Twilight, unbeloved of men,
Creep hand in hand from yon obscurest glen.

They breathe their spells towards the departing day,
Encompassing the earth, air, stars, and sea;
Light, sound, and motion, own the potent sway,
Responding to the charm with its own mystery.
The winds are still, or the dry church-tower grass
Knows not their gentle motions as they pass.

Thou too, aerial pile, whose pinnacles
Point from one shrine like pyramids of fire,
Obey'st I in silence their sweet solemn spells,
Clothing in hues of heaven thy dim and distant spire,
Around whose lessening and invisible height
Gather among the stars the clouds of night.

The dead are sleeping in their sepulchres:
· And, mouldering as they sleep, a thrilling sound,
Half sense half thought, among the darkness stirs,
Breathed from their wormy beds all living things around,
And, mingling with the still night and mute sky,
Its awful hush is felt inaudibly.

Thus solemnized and softened, death is mild
And terrorless as this serenest night.
Here could I hope, like some enquiring child
Sporting on graves, that death did hide from human sight
Sweet secrets, or beside its breathless sleep
That loveliest dreams perpetual watch did keep.

PERCY BYSSHE SHELLEY, 'A SUMMER EVENING
CHURCHYARD, LECHLADE, GLOUCESTERSHIRE'

# September

Thank God! we are not only at peace, but in full plenty – nay, and in full beauty too... The apple and walnut-trees bend down with fruit, as in a poetic description of Paradise.

HORACE WALPOLE

My eyes are full, my silent heart is stirred,
Amid these days so bright
Of ceaseless warmth and light;
Summer that will not die,
Autumn, without one sigh
O'er sweet hours passing by –
Cometh that tender note
Out of thy tiny throat,
Like grief, or love, insisting to be heard,
O little plaintive bird!

No need of word
Well know I all your tale – forgotten bird!
Soon you and I together
Must face the winter weather,
Remembering how we sung
Our primrose fields among,
In days when life was young;
Now, all is growing old,
And the warm earth's a-cold,
Still, with brave heart we'll sing on, little bird,
Sing only. Not one word.

DINAH M. MULOCK CRAIK, 'A SEPTEMBER ROBIN'

# September 1

They say that there are a prodigious number of birds hereabouts this year, so that perhaps *I* may kill a few.

Jane Austen (1796)

# September 2

Set out about eleven for Canterbury. The road very hilly, but through a most rich country of orchards, hop-grounds and pastures, villages and pretty houses, with lawns and gardens frequently occurring.

Ann Ward Radcliffe (1797)

# September 3

We have, as usual, beat all the country hollow; but the shooting is sheer slavery. The ground like hot cinders, the heat like India, and getting a point out of the question. All must be done by walking the barren lands with both barrels cocked, and popping at all distances the moment the birds top the stubble. We all came home so exhausted as scarcely to be able to move.

Colonel Peter Hawker (1835)

## September 4

Freshwater. Mrs Carter's lodging. Very fine and sunny. To Farringford, meet William with the ponies. Breakfast, then out to croquet-lawn, sit in shade, reading odd numbers of a Conservative magazine. A. T. comes, friendly; says, 'I saw a beast watching me! I saw his legs behind the ilex.'

William Allingham (1868)

## September 5

Dug the fruit border the fourth time after a great rain: it fell well to pieces, & seems to be well-mellow'd with sand & lime: till this rain it lay in great Clods as hard as stones, being so much trod by the masons, & harden'd by a hot, sunny Summer. It has three coats of good mould on it, & must be full two feet deep on good soil.

Gilbert White (1761)

# September 6

At one o'clock I eat a bit of cold rost Beef for Dinner and then I took my Mare and went to Shepton Mallett, put up my Mare at the George Inn, and walked down to Mr Wickhams House, but he and his Wife are at Wells. I left a Note at the House for him, wherein I told him that I must leave the Curacy of Cary at Michaelmas. I then went & spent the whole Afternoon at Mr Whites with Mrs White and my dear Betsy White.

James Woodforde (1773)

# September 7

Went to the Farm, drank whey in the dairy, paid Jacob Knight £2 2s for the use of the cricket ground on the Common, and took a game fowl's egg to Elizabeth Knight. As I returned I heard in Greenway Lane the old familiar sound once so common, the sound of the flail on the barn floor. I had not heard it for years. I looked in at the barn door and found a man threshing out his barley.

Francis Kilvert (1874)

# September 8

The wasps (which are without number this dry hot summer) attack the grapes in a grievous manner. Hung-up 16 bottles with treacle, & beer, which make great havock among them. Bagged about fifty of the best bunches in Crape-bags. Some of the forwardest bunches are very eatable, tho' not curiously ripe. Mr Snooke's grapes were eat naked to the stones fortnight ago, when they were quite green.

There are about 3 braces of second-crop Succades, which will come in good time if the weather proves good.

Frequent showers since the 4 th of Aug: now a promise of dry weather. The fields abound with grass as if there had been no drought this summer.

Gilbert White (1762)

# September 9

Hartley Coleridge then took us to the Rydal waterfalls and told us stories of the proprietors, the Fleming family. One of the falls, or forces as they call them here, was the most perfect I had ever seen. Our poet's recognition of the perpetual poetry in Nature was very inspiring and inspiriting.

Caroline Fox (1837)

## September 10

We finished harvest this Afternoon, and thank God! had a fine Time for it, & all well. Sent a Note this Morning early by Briton to Mr Anson at Lyng, to desire his and Brothers Company to dinner on Wednesday next, had a genteel Answer back, but they are engaged. Bidwell's Folks, got the Newspapers for us.

James Woodforde (1796)

# September 11

We have got a codicil to summer, that is as delightful as, I believe, the seasons in the Fortunate Islands. It is pity it lasts but till seven in the evening, and then one remains with a black chimney for five hours. I wish the sun was not so fashionable as never to come into the country till autumn and the shooting season; as if Niobe's children were not hatched and fledged before the first of September.

Horace Walpole (1791)

# September 12

Thank God! we are not only at peace, but in full plenty – nay, and in full beauty too... The apple and walnut-trees bend down with fruit, as in a poetic description of Paradise.

Horace Walpole (1788)

# September 13

Sunday was a bright and hot day, and in the forenoon I set out on a walk, not well knowing whither, over a very dusty road, with not a particle of shade along its dead level. The Welsh mountains were before me, at the distance of three or four miles, – long ridgy hills, descending pretty abruptly upon the plain; on either side of the road, here and there, an old whitewashed, thatched stone cottage, or a stone farm-house, with an aspect of some antiquity.

Nathaniel Hawthorne (1854)

# September 14

Sandhills – fine; ride pony, Lea Park, moor near Hammer Pond; meet boys, one of whom lifts hand with switch in it to Jenny's nose. She starts violently, flings me off and kicks left arm – gallops off. Back and arm hurt.

William Allingham (1888)

Season of mists and mellow fruitfulness,
Close bosom-friend of the maturing sun;
Conspiring with him how to load and bless
With fruit the vines that round the thatch-eaves run;
To bend with apples the moss'd cottage-trees,
And fill all fruit with ripeness to the core;
To swell the gourd, and plump the hazel shells
With a sweet kernel; to set budding more,
And still more, later flowers for the bees,
Until they think warm days will never cease,
For Summer has o'er-brimm'd their clammy cells.

Who hath not seen thee oft amid thy store?
Sometimes whoever seeks abroad may find
Thee sitting careless on a granary floor,
Thy hair soft-lifted by the winnowing wind;
Or on a half-reap'd furrow sound asleep,
Drows'd with the fume of poppies, while thy hook
Spares the next swath and all its twined flowers:
And sometimes like a gleaner thou dost keep
Steady thy laden head across a brook;
Or by a cider-press, with patient look,
Thou watchest the last oozings hours by hours.

Where are the songs of Spring? Ay, where are they?
Think not of them, thou hast thy music too, –
While barred clouds bloom the soft-dying day,
And touch the stubble-plains with rosy hue;
Then in a wailful choir the small gnats mourn
Among the river sallows, borne aloft
Or sinking as the light wind lives or dies;
And full-grown lambs loud bleat from hilly bourn;
Hedge-crickets sing; and now with treble soft
The red-breast whistles from a garden-croft;
And gathering swallows twitter in the skies.

JOHN KEATS, 'TO AUTUMN'

# September 15

Observed the great half moon setting behind the mountain ridge, and watched the shapes its various segments presented as it slowly sunk – first the foot of a boot, all but the heel – then a little pyramid – then a star of the first magnitude – indeed, it was not distinguishable from the evening star at its largest – then rapidly a smaller, a small, a very small star – and, as it diminished in size, so it grew paler in tint. And now where is it? Unseen – but a little fleecy cloud hangs above the main ridge, and is rich in amber light.

Samuel Taylor Coleridge (1801)

## September 16

Out in the Bay dredging for Echinoderms with 'Carrots.' Brilliantly fine. The hail was a failure, but being out in a boat on a waveless sea under a cloudless sky, I was scarcely depressed at this!

W. N. P. Barbellion (1912)

## September 17

Up, and my father being gone to bed ill last night and continuing so this morning, I was forced to come to a new consideration, whether it was fit for to let my uncle and his son go to Wisbeach about my uncle Day's estate alone or no, and concluded it unfit; and so resolved to go with them myself, leaving my wife there, I begun a journey with them, and with much ado, through the fens, along dikes, where sometimes we were ready to have our horses sink to the belly, we got by night, with great deal of stir and hard riding, to Parson's Drove...

Samuel Pepys (1663)

## September 18

What dreadful hot weather we have! It keeps one in a continual state of inelegance.

Jane Austen (1796)

## September 19

It was a still warm day of late summer, but a diviner radiance lay over garden field, and wood for me. I determined I would not speak to my mother till after I had received my answer.

After breakfast I went out to the garden – the flowers seemed to smile and nod their heads at me, leaning with a kind of tender brilliance to greet me; in a thick bush I heard the flute-notes of my favourite thrush – the brisk chirruping of the sparrows came from the ivied gable.

A. C. Benson (1900)

# September 20

The day was cloudy and lowering, and there were several little spatterings of rain, while we rambled about. The two children ran shouting hither and thither, and were continually clambering into dangerous places, racing along ledges of broken wall. At last they altogether disappeared for a good while; their voices, which had heretofore been plainly audible, were hushed, nor was there any answer when we began to call them, while making ready for our departure. But they finally appeared, coming out of the moat, where they had been picking and eating blackberries, – which, they said, grew very plentifully there, and which they were very reluctant to leave. Before quitting the castle, I must not forget the ivy, which makes a perfect tapestry over a large portion of the walls.

Nathaniel Hawthorne (1854)

# September 21

Sweet fresh morning. Left Cobham between seven and eight. Passed under a picturesque bridge uniting the grounds of Paine's hill; high, tough, broken banks, topped with lofty trees, that hang over a light rustic bridge.

Ann Ward Radcliffe (1798)

## September 22

Bee stalls are very heavy this year: this hot dry summer has proved advantageous to bees.

Vast N. *Aurora*, very red, & coping over in the zenith.

Gilbert White (1778)

## September 23

I breakfasted, dined, supped & slept at Parsonage. It rained almost the whole Day, & I did not stir out at all.

James Woodforde (1772)

## September 24

Mary first met us in the avenue. She looked so fat and well that we were made very happy by the sight of her; then came Sara, and last of all Joanna. Tom was forking corn, standing upon the corn cart. We dressed ourselves immediately and got tea.

Dorothy Wordsworth (1802)

# September 25

This morning I set off, in rather a drizzling rain, from Kensington, on horseback, accompanied by my son, with an intention of going to Uphusband, near Andover, which is situated in the North West corner of Hampshire. It is very true that I could have gone to Uphusband by travelling only about 66 miles, and in the space of about eight hours. But my object was not to see inns and turnpike-roads, but to see the *country*; to see the farmers at home, and to see the labourers in the fields; and to do this you must go either on foot or on horse-back.

William Cobbett (1822)

# September 26

The Sucado-melons now come apace.
 Vast rains, thunder & lightening for 8 to 10 days; & a likelihood of great floods.
 Grapes in great plenty, & perfection.

Gilbert White (1760)

## September 27

To Beddington, that ancient seat of the Carews, a fine old hall, but a scambling house, famous for the first orange garden in England, being now overgrown trees, planted in the ground and secured in winter with a wooden tabernacle and stoves. This seat is rarely watered, lying low, and environed with good pastures. The pomegranates bear here.

John Evelyn (1658)

## September 28

I cast regretful glances of memory back to my garden at Boulge, which I want to see dug up and replanted. I have bought anemone roots which in the Spring shall blow Tyrian dyes, and Irises of a newer and more brilliant prism than Noah saw in the clouds.

Edward Fitzgerald (1844)

# September 29

Then in the evening, towards night, it fell to thunder, lighten, and rain so violently that my house was all afloat, and I in all the rain up to the gutters, and there dabbled in the rain and wet half an hour, enough to have killed a man.

Samuel Pepys (1663)

# September 30

We, who live always encompassed by rural scenery, can afford to be stationary; though we ourselves, were I not too closely engaged with Homer, should perhaps follow your example, and seek a little refreshment from variety and change of place, – a course that we might find not only agreeable, but, after a sameness of thirteen years, perhaps useful.

William Cowper (1786)

Come, Sons of Summer, by whose toil
We are the lords of wine and oil:
By whose tough labours, and rough hands,
We rip up first, then reap our lands.
Crown'd with the ears of corn, now come,
And, to the pipe, sing Harvest Home.

Come forth, my lord, and see the cart
Drest up with all the country art.
See, here a maukin, there a sheet,
As spotless pure, as it is sweet:
The horses, mares, and frisking fillies,
Clad, all, in linen white as lilies.
The harvest swains and wenches bound
For joy, to see the Hock-Cart crown'd.

ROBERT HERRICK, FROM
'THE HOCK-CART, OR HARVEST HOME'

# *October*

To-day we had one of those soft, still, dreamy,
golden afternoons peculiar to Autumn.

FRANCIS KILVERT

The green elm with the one great bough of gold
Lets leaves into the grass slip, one by one, –
The short hill grass, the mushrooms small milk-white,
Harebell and scabious and tormentil,
That blackberry and gorse, in dew and sun,
Bow down to; and the wind travels too light
To shake the fallen birch leaves from the fern;
The gossamers wander at their own will.
At heavier steps than birds' the squirrels scold.
The rich scene has grown fresh again and new
As Spring and to the touch is not more cool
Than it is warm to the gaze; and now I might
As happy be as earth is beautiful,
Were I some other or with earth could turn
In alternation of violet and rose,
Harebell and snowdrop, at their season due,
And gorse that has no time not to be gay.
But if this be not happiness, – who knows?
Some day I shall think this a happy day,
And this mood by the name of melancholy
Shall no more blackened and obscured be.

EDWARD THOMAS, 'OCTOBER'

# October 1

Once more we are back in the month when the robin sings so much. The robins, I find, are the tamest of all the birds in the garden; and as we fork over the beds, or dig new ones, they follow us all about, enjoying much the newly turned-up earth.

Mrs C. W. Earle (1896)

# October 2

My affectionate respects attend Mrs Hill. She has put Mr Wright to the expense of building a new hot-house: the plants produced by the seeds she gave me, having grown so large as to require an apartment by themselves.

William Cowper (1779)

# October 3

Glided smoothly under a light summer air; the evening splendid, and the scene most lovely. The Needles are vast dark blocks of rock, tall, but not pointed, standing out from the island in the sea.

Ann Ward Radcliffe (1800)

# October 4

In the forenoon I walked down in the park to look at an old pollard, from whence a swarm of bees had been taken. In the even, went down to Jones's, to make up the following trifling affair. Some time in the summer, Master Ball and a little boy of Riche's found a swarm of bees in Halland Park, which they agreed to divide between them, and they sent a person to Mr Gibbs, to ask his consent to take the bees at the proper time for taking them. The fellow never saw Mr Gibbs, but told them Mr Gibbs gave his free consent. They, knowing no other than that they had the keeper's free consent, innocently enough proceeded to action.

Thomas Turner (1758)

# October 5

It rained almost all day on Wednesday, so that I did not go out till late in the afternoon, and then only took a stroll along Oxford Street and Holborn, and back through Fleet Street and the Strand. Yesterday, at a little after ten, I went to the ambassador's to get my wife's passport for Lisbon.

Nathaniel Hawthorne (1855)

# October 6

Grapes do not ripen: they are as backward as in the bad summer 1782. The crop is large.

Some hirundines.

Timothy the tortoise is very dull, & never stirs from the border of the fruit-wall. Many loads of hops set-out for wey hill.

Gilbert White (1789)

# October 7

At Uphusband, a little village in a deep dale, about five miles to the North of Andover, and about three miles to the South of the Hills at Highclere. The wheat is sown here, and up, and, as usual, at this time of the year, looks very beautiful. The wages of the labourers brought down to six shillings a week! a horrible thing to think of; but, I hear, it is still worse in Wiltshire.

William Cobbett (1822)

## October 8

Fine still weather in general since thee 9th September now rain, & a vast storm of wind, that blew-down some shrubs, & beat to pieces all the flowers.

Gilbert White (1758)

## October 9

My Man Robin Emett, set out this Morning for Ansforde. I was very bad all last night and all this day, having got a bad boil upon my Posteriors. Dined in the B.C.R. Went to bed this Evening very soon, being worse a good deal.

James Woodforde (1761)

## October 10

I am now returned to my dull home here after my usual
pottering about in the midland counties of England. A little
Bedfordshire – a little Northamptonshire – a little more
folding of the hands – the same faces – the same fields – the
same thoughts occurring at the same turns of road – this is
all I have to tell of; nothing at all added – but the summer
gone. My garden is covered with yellow and brown leaves;
and a man is digging up the garden beds before my window,
and will plant some roots and bulbs for next year.

Edward Fitzgerald (1844)

## October 11

It should be mentioned, that, in the morning, before embarking S— and the children on board the steamer, I saw a fragment of a rainbow among the clouds, and remembered the old adage bidding 'sailors take warning'. In the afternoon, as J— and I were railing from Southampton, we saw another fragmentary rainbow, which, by the same adage, should be the 'sailor's delight'. The weather has rather tended to confirm the first omen, but the sea-captains tell me that the steamer must have gone beyond the scope of these winds.

Nathaniel Hawthorne (1855)

## October 12

If one can depend on any season, it is on the chill suns of October, which, like an elderly beauty, are less capricious than spring or summer. Our old-fashioned October, you know, reached eleven days into modern November, and I still depend on that reckoning, when I have a mind to protract the year.

Horace Walpole (1771)

# October 13

About five miles from Salisbury, gain the summit of a high ridge, and look at once upon a new and grander ridge large and sharper hills rising to a great extent, with the vast Cathedral and lofty spire of Salisbury in front.

Ann Ward Radcliffe (1801)

# October 14

Keyhaven. Left here by way of pleasant conveyance in a yacht. Wind changed, carried away mizen-boom. Heaviest sea known for a long time off Calshot. Gentlemen all sick and wet through with a happy mixture of rain and breakers, and a foul gale in our teeth.

Colonel Peter Hawker (1829)

# October 15

This cold weather comes very fortunately for Edward's nerves, with such a house full; it suits him exactly; he is all alive and cheerful. Poor James, on the contrary, must be running his toes into the fire.

Jane Austen (1813)

O Autumn, laden with fruit, and stain'd
With the blood of the grape, pass not, but sit
Beneath my shady roof; there thou may'st rest,
And tune thy jolly voice to my fresh pipe,
And all the daughters of the year shall dance!
Sing now the lusty song of fruits and flowers.

'The narrow bud opens her beauties to
The sun, and love runs in her thrilling veins;
Blossoms hang round the brows of Morning, and
Flourish down the bright cheek of modest Eve,
Till clust'ring Summer breaks forth into singing,
And feather'd clouds strew flowers round her head.

'The spirits of the air live in the smells
Of fruit; and Joy, with pinions light, roves round
The gardens, or sits singing in the trees.'
Thus sang the jolly Autumn as he sat,
Then rose, girded himself, and o'er the bleak
Hills fled from our sight; but left his golden load.

WILLIAM BLAKE, 'TO AUTUMN'

# October 16

Saw little Alamayu in the road; two of the De Havilland children came up, whom he kissed, and then came the snuffy old Postman with his bag, and the little Prince kissed him too – partly, perhaps, as an important functionary who often bears tidings of interest. Breakfast at Miss Thackeray's, enlivened by the children. Walker is going in with a little picture of a Girl watering flowers.

Walk to Yarmouth and cross to Lymington; back in the afternoon; roughish sea and coldish on the coach. Myrtle Cottage. Dine at Miss Thackeray's; the Miss Ritchies, F. Walker. Talk of George Eliot, etc. F. W. and I have cigarettes and then to drawing-room, where I read aloud Shelley's Sonnet 'Being your Slave', and Leigh Hunt's 'Abou Ben Adhem'. We fall to drawing pigs with our eyes shut and dawdle away time till 12 o'clock.

William Allingham (1868)

# October 17

It seems to me (but I believe it seems so every year) that our trees keep their leaves very long; I suppose, because of no severe frosts or winds up to this time. And my garden still shows some Geranium, Salvia, Nasturtium, Great Convolvulus, and that grand African Marigold whose Colour is so comfortable to us Spanish-like Paddies. I have also a dear Oleander which even now has a score of blossoms on it, and touches the top of my little Green-house; having been sent me when *'haut comme ça,'* as Marquis Somebody used to say in the days of Louis XIV. Don't you love the Oleander? So clean in its leaves and stem, as so beautiful in its flower; loving to stand in water which it drinks up so fast. I rather worship mine.

Edward Fitzgerald (1882)

# October 18

Pray tell grandmamma that we have begun getting seeds for her; I hope we shall be able to get her a nice collection, but I am afraid this wet weather is very much against them. How glad I am to hear she has had such good success with her chickens, but I wish there had been more bantams amongst them.

Jane Austen (1813)

# October 19

Left Steephill. Sailed from Cowes in the Southampton packet, about half-past five; the Naiad frigate lying before the town. What particularly struck me in the passage was, not only the sun actually appearing to set in the sea, but the splendid amber light, left upon that long level perspective of waters, and the vessels upon it at various distances, seeming dark on this side, and marking out its extent to the eye.

Ann Ward Radcliffe (1811)

# October 20

From the road before the lawn, people used plainly to see the topmasts of the men-of-war lying in Hollesley bay during the war. I like the idea of this: the old English house holding up its enquiring chimneys and weather cocks (there is great physiognomy in weathercocks) toward the far-off sea, and the ships upon it. How well I remember when we used all to be in the Nursery, and from the window see the hounds come across the lawn, my Father and Mr Jenney in their hunting caps, etc., with their long whips – all Daguerreotyped into the mind's eye now – and that is all.

Edward Fitzgerald (1839)

# October 21

Your pictures shall be sent as soon as any of us go to London, but I think that will not be till the Parliament meets. Can we easily leave the remains of such a year as this? It is still all gold. I have not dined or gone to bed by a fire till the day before yesterday. Instead of the glorious and ever-memorable year 1759, as the newspapers call it, I call it this ever-warm and victorious year. We have not had more conquest than fine weather: one would think we had plundered East and West Indies of sunshine.

Horace Walpole (1759)

# October 22

All the mountains black and tremendously obscure, except Swinside. At this time I saw, one after the other, nearly in the same place, two perfect moon-rainbows, the one foot in the field below my garden, the other in the field nearest but two to the church. It was grey-moonlight-mist-colour.

Samuel Taylor Coleridge (1801)

## October 23

Very fine; in the New Forest. Holmsley – path to Burley, field-lane fern-banked, delightful. Hamlet on its gorsey common, a big oak among the hollies.

William Allingham (1863)

## October 24

Edward and George came to us soon after seven on Saturday, very well, but very cold, having by choice travelled on the outside, and with no great coat but what Mr Wise, the coachman, good-naturedly spared them of his, as they sat by his side. They were so much chilled when they arrived, that I was afraid they must have taken cold; but it does not seem at all the case; I never saw them looking better.

Jane Austen (1808)

## October 25

We have been exceedingly busy ever since you went away. In the first place we have had to rejoice two or three times every day at your having such delightful weather for the whole of your journey, and in the second place we have been obliged to take advantage of the very delightful weather ourselves by going to see almost all our neighbours.

Jane Austen (1800)

## October 26

We are afraid that our Maid, Molly, is with Child she looks so big, but she denies it very positively.

James Woodforde (1794)

# October 27

I have rarely seen Langley Church and Churchyard look more beautiful than they did this morning. The weather was lovely and round the quiet Church the trees were gorgeous, the elms dazzling golden and the beeches burning crimson. The golden elms illuminated the Church and Churchyard with strong yellow light and the beeches flamed and glowed with scarlet and crimson fire like the Burning Bush. The place lay quiet in the still autumn sunshine. Then the latch of the wicket of the wicket gate tinkled and pretty Keren Wood appeared coming along the Church path under the spreading boughs of the wide larch, and in the glare of yellow light the bell broke solemnly through the golden elms that stood stately round the Church.

To-day we had one of those soft, still, dreamy, golden afternoons peculiar to Autumn.

Francis Kilvert (1872)

# October 28

Up at 7 – fog. Drive to Christchurch, the sun breaking through the fog.

William Allingham (1864)

## October 29

Going to London, my Lord Mayor's show stopped me in Cheapside; one of the pageants represented a great wood, with the royal oak, and history of his Majesty's miraculous escape at Boscobel.

John Evelyn (1660)

## October 30

Fog that you might cut with a knife all the way from London to Newbury. This fog does not wet things. It is rather a smoke than a fog.

William Cobbett (1821)

# October 31

The full moon glided behind a black cloud. And what then? and who cared? It was past seven o'clock in the morning. There is a small cloud in the east, not larger than the moon and ten times brighter than she! So passes night, and all her favours vanish in our minds ungrateful!

Samuel Taylor Coleridge (1803)

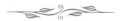

The wild duck startles like a sudden thought,
And heron slow as if it might be caught.
The flopping crows on weary wings go by
And grey beard jackdaws noising as they fly.
The crowds of starnels whizz and hurry by,
And darken like a clod the evening sky.
The larks like thunder rise and suthy round,
Then drop and nestle in the stubble ground.
The wild swan hurries hight and noises loud
With white neck peering to the evening clowd.
The weary rooks to distant woods are gone.
With lengths of tail the magpie winnows on
To neighbouring tree, and leaves the distant crow
While small birds nestle in the edge below.

JOHN CLARE, 'AUTUMN BIRDS'

# *November*

There is a heavy dun fog on the river and over the
city to-day, the very gloomiest atmosphere that ever
I was acquainted with... There are lamps burning in
the counting-rooms and lobbies of the warehouses,
and they gleam distinctly through the windows.

NATHANIEL HAWTHORNE

Than these November skies
Is no sky lovelier. The clouds are deep;
Into their gray the subtle spies
Of colour creep,
Changing that high austerity to delight,
Till even the leaden interfolds are bright.
And, where the cloud breaks, faint far azure peers
Ere a thin flushing cloud again
Shuts up that loveliness, or shares.
The huge great clouds move slowly, gently, as
Reluctant the quick sun should shine in vain,
Holding in bright caprice their rain.
And when of colours none,
Not rose, nor amber, nor the scarce late green,
Is truly seen, –
In all the myriad gray,
In silver height and dusky deep, remain
The loveliest,
Faint purple flushes of the unvanquished sun.

JOHN FREEMAN, 'NOVEMBER SKIES'

# November 1

Rev Wm Barnes comes on my invitation to give a lecture at the Literary Institution. He duly arrives by train at 3, and I gladly welcome the good old poet. We walk about the Town and he shows much interest in the Furniture Broker's shop, old china, pictures, etc. – and bargains for a little oil-painting. Aïdé arrives, whom I have invited to meet Barnes. I take them for a walk to Buckland Rings, supposed ancient British Camp; then dinner at my lodging (which I hope went off tolerably), and we moved to the Lecture Room.

William Allingham (1864)

# November 2

The morning was dull, thick and gloomy, threatening rain, but just before we got into Bath a sunbeam stole across the world and lighted the Queen of the West with the ethereal beauty of a fairy city, while all the land blazed gorgeous with the brilliant and many coloured trees. Almost in a moment the dull dark leaden sky was replaced by a sheet of brilliant blue and the lovely city shone dazzling and lustrous upon the hill sides, her palaces veiled with a tender mist and softened by delicate gleams of pearl and blue.

Francis Kilvert (1874)

# November 3

It's full moon with a vengeance to-night. Out of the front door a field of big turnips, and beyond, a spiky wood, with red bands of light behind it. Out of the back door an old tree with just a leaf or two remaining and a moon perched in the branches.

Katherine Mansfield (1914)

# November 4

After breakfast I drove Nancy over to Witchingham being fine Morn' to Mr Jeans's and spent the remaining part of the Morn' with him & his Wife. We met with Mr Jeans in our Parish coming to us. Mrs Jeans is far advanced in pregnancy. We stayed there till almost 2 o'clock, they pressed us much to dine with them, but there being no Moon and likewise some Rain falling we could not, but borrowed an Umbrella and Mr Jeans's French Cloke for Nancy & returned home by three o'clock. It rained tho' very gently all the way. Dinner to day Knuckle of Veal boiled & Pigs face and a Neck of Pork rosted with apple sauce. Mrs Jeans was pressing for us to dine with them more than was agreeable. It was rather beyond the Line of being pleasing.

James Woodforde (1794)

# November 5

This being the 5th of November, is the worst of all days in the year for letter-writing. Continually called upon to remember the bonfire, one is apt to forget every thing else. The boys at Olney have likewise a very entertaining sport, which commences annually upon this day. They call it Hockey; and it consist in dashing each other with mud, and the windows also, so that I am forced to rise now and then, and to threaten them with a horsewhip to preserve our own.

William Cowper (1785)

# November 6

We had delightful weather when I first got home; but on the fourth morning Dorothy roused me from my sleep with, 'It is time to get up, Aunt, it is a *blasty* morning, it *does blast* so'; and the next morning, not more encouraging to me, she says, 'It is a *haily* morning, it hails so hard!'

Dorothy Wordsworth (1810)

## November 7

Left London at eleven and got to Keyhaven at eleven. Of course I changed the weathercock. The wind had been all the week north-east, and I turned the cock to south-west and rain before I reached Winchester. There had been birds, and Read had had some sport.

Colonel Peter Hawker (1835)

## November 8

Do you plant without rain as I do, in order to have your trees die, that you may have the pleasure of planting them over again with rain? Have you any Mrs Clive that pulls down barns that intercept your prospect; or have you any Lord Radnor that plants trees to intercept his own prospect, that he may cut them down again to make an alteration?

Horace Walpole (1752)

# November 9

The town, with lighted windows and noise of the clogged passengers in the streets – sound of the unseen river. Mountains scarcely perceivable except by eyes long used to them, and supported by the images of memory glowing in on the impulses of immediate impression. On the sky, black clouds' two or three dim, untwinkling stars, like full stops on damp paper, and large stains and spreads of sullen white, like a tunic of white wool seen here and there through a torn and tattered cloak of black. Whence do these stains of white proceed all over the sky, so long after sunset, and from their indifference of place in the sky, seemingly unaffected by the west?

Samuel Taylor Coleridge (1803)

# November 10

Poor C. left us, and we came home together. We left Keswick at 2 o'clock and did not arrive at Grasmere till 9 o'clock. I burnt myself with Coleridge's aquafortis. C. had a sweet day for his ride. Every sight and every sound reminded me of him – dear, dear fellow, of his many talks to us, by day and by night, of all dear things.

Dorothy Wordsworth (1801)

# November 11

Most uncommon frost for one night, & considering the season of the Year: Ice near an inch thick, & the dirt hard enough to bear an Horse.

Gilbert White (1755)

# November 12

One to whom fish is so welcome as it is to me, can have no great occasion to distinguish the sorts. In general, therefore, whatever fish are likely to think a jaunt into the country agreeable, will be sure to find me ready to receive them; butts, plaice, flounder or any other.

William Cowper (1776)

# November 13

It has been blowing here tremendously for a fortnight, but to-day is like a spring day, and plenty of roses are growing over the labourers' cottages. The Great Eastern lies at her moorings beyond the window where I write these words; looks very dull and unpromising. A dark column of smoke from Chatham Dockyard, where the iron shipbuilding is in progress, has a greater significance in it, I fancy.

Charles Dickens (1865)

# November 14

There is a heavy dun fog on the river and over the city to-day, the very gloomiest atmosphere that ever I was acquainted with. On the river the steamboats strike gongs or ring bells to give warning of their approach. There are lamps burning in the counting-rooms and lobbies of the warehouses, and they gleam distinctly through the windows.

Nathaniel Hawthorne (1853)

The boy, that scareth from the spiry wheat
The melancholy crow – in hurry weaves,
Beneath an ivied tree, his sheltering seat,
Of rushy flags and sedges tied in sheaves,
Or from the field a shock of stubble thieves.
There he doth dithering sit, and entertain
His eyes with marking the storm-driven leaves;
Oft spying nests where he spring eggs had ta'en,
And wishing in his heart 'twas summer-time again.

Thus wears the month along, in checker'd moods,
Sunshine and shadows, tempests loud, and calms;
One hour dies silent o'er the sleepy woods,
The next wakes loud with unexpected storms;
A dreary nakedness the field deforms –
Yet many a rural sound, and rural sight,
Lives in the village still about the farms,
Where toil's rude uproar hums from morn till night
Noises, in which the ears of Industry delight.

At length the stir of rural labour's still,
And Industry her care awhile forgoes;
When Winter comes in earnest to fulfil
His yearly task, at bleak November's close,
And stops the plough, and hides the field in snows;
When frost locks up the stream in chill delay,
And mellows on the hedge the jetty sloes,
For little birds – then Toil hath time for play,
And nought but threshers' flails awake the dreary day.

JOHN CLARE, FROM 'NOVEMBER'

## November 15

About Noon (being fine) I walked out a coursing taking only Briton and the Boy with me, Ben being in Weston Great Field plowing. We stayed out till near 4 o'clock, saw no Hare but coursed one Rabbit and killed it. We walked over most of the large Brakes of Ringland. Nancy very busy with the Maids all the Morning in making some black Pudding &c.

James Woodforde (1791)

## November 16

A foggy breeze, which about four turned to a drizzling rain. Weathered it from that time till dark, and came in with 12 wigeon. Birds extremely wild, as they always are in foggy weather. Nearest of my two shots – about 140 yards.

Colonel Peter Hawker (1844)

# November 17

What fine weather this is! Not very becoming perhaps early in the morning, but very pleasant out of doors at noon, and very wholesome – at least everybody fancies so, and imagination is everything.

Jane Austen (1798)

# November 18

The weather cleared up, and the Queen has just returned from a walk. She hopes Lord Melbourne got safe to London in spite of the wet and the water on the road; and she hopes he will take great care of himself. She would be thankful if he would let her know to-morrow if he will dine with her also on Thursday or not.

Queen Victoria (1839)

## November 19

A thorough wet day, the only day the greater part of which I have not spent out of doors since I left home.

William Cobbett (1821)

## November 20

Hacker has been here to-day putting in the fruit trees. A new plan has been suggested concerning the plantation of the new inclosure of the right-hand side of the elm walk: the doubt is whether it would be better to make a little orchard of it by planting apples, pears, and cherries, or whether it should be larch, mountain ash, and acacia.

Jane Austen (1800)

# November 21

I breakfasted, dined, supped & slept again at home. Bill breakfasted, dined, supped & slept here again. Was very ill going to bed again last Night, I don't know the reason of it unless it be eating hash Mutton done in a Copper Sauce Pan on Wednesday last, or being made uneasy by my suspicions of Bill. Recd a Letter from Bathurst & one in it for Mr Wilson Junr. Recd of a Neighbour for 2 small Piggs 0.10.0. Bill was very saucy this Evening & said that he never did any harm in his Life, & after all that has passed. I told my Maid Betty this morning that the other Maid Nanny looked so big about the Waist that I was afraid she was with Child, but Betty told me she thought not, but would soon inform me if it is so.

James Woodforde (1779)

# November 22

When I came to town I found that herrings were out of season: but sprats, which Ray says are undoubtedly young herrings, abounded in such quantities, that in these hard times they were a great help to the poor. Cods & haddocks in plenty: smelts beginning to come in.

The public papers have abounded with accounts of most severe & early frosts, not only in the more Northern parts of Europe, but on the Rhine, & in Holland. The news of severe weather usually reaches us some days before the cold arrives; which most times follows soon when we hear of rigorous cold on the Continent.

Gilbert White (1774)

# November 23

The winter sets in with great severity. The rigour of the season, and the advanced price of grain, are very threatening to the poor. It is well with those that can feed upon a promise, and wrap themselves up warm in the robe of salvation.

William Cowper (1782)

## November 24

Gathered-in all the grapes for fear of the frost.

We have now enjoyed a dry, good season, with no more rain than has been useful, ever since the first week in August.

Gilbert White (1777)

## November 25

On a sudden impulse I walked up from Sandhills about 3 o'clock, to call at Aldworth, the roads greasy with a thaw, ice on pools. On Blackdown met Hallam, and then Tennyson. They hospitably determined that I was to stay the night, and would telegraph Witley accordingly.

William Allingham (1884)

## November 26

We continue to tack the vines, & peaches &c.

A man brought me a common sea-gull alive: three crows had got it down in a field, & were endeavouring to demolish it.

Gilbert White (1776)

# November 27

My Brother recommending me last Night to carry a small Piece of the roll Brimstone sewed up in a piece of very thin Linnen, to bed with me and if I felt any Symptom of the Cramp to hold it in my hand or put it near the affected part, which I did, as I apprehended at one time it was coming into one of my legs, and I felt no more advances of it. This I thought deserving of notice, even in so trifling a book as this.

James Woodforde (1789)

# November 28

The woods & hedges are beautifully fringed with snow.
    Ordered Thomas carefully to beat-off the snow that lodges on the South side of the laurels & laurustines. Snow covers the ground. Snow melts on the roofs against the sun.

Gilbert White (1782)

# November 29

When we consider that a whole sky, through all the seasons, is open to one vale, with its stars and sun and moon and clouds of all measures and manners and colours, what more can an immortal mind desire?

James Smetham (1871)

# November 30

I came over the high hill on the south of Guildford, and came down to Chilworth, and up the valley to Albury. I noticed, in my first Rural Ride, this beautiful valley, its hangers, its meadows, its hop-gardens, and its ponds. This valley of Chilworth has great variety, and is very pretty; but after seeing Hawkley, every other place loses in point of beauty and interest. This pretty valley of Chilworth has a run of water which comes out of the high hills, and which, occasionally, spreads into a pond; so that there is in fact a series of ponds connected by this run of water.

William Cobbett (1822)

No sun – no moon!
No morn – no noon –
No dawn – no dusk – no proper time of day.
No warmth, no cheerfulness, no healthful ease,
No comfortable feel in any member –
No shade, no shine, no butterflies, no bees,
No fruits, no flowers, no leaves, no birds! –
November!

THOMAS HOOD, 'NOVEMBER'

# *December*

While snow the window-panes bedim,
The fire curls up a sunny charm,
Where, creaming o'er the pitcher's rim,
The flowering ale is set to warm.

John Clare

Tho' now no more the musing ear
Delights to listen to the breeze
That lingers o'er the green wood shade,
I love thee Winter! well.

Sweet are the harmonies of Spring,
Sweet is the summer's evening gale,
Pleasant the autumnal winds that shake
The many-colour'd grove.

And pleasant to the sober'd soul
The silence of the wintry scene,
When Nature shrouds her in her trance

Not undelightful now to roam
The wild heath sparkling on the sight;
Not undelightful now to pace
The forest's ample rounds;

And see the spangled branches shine,
And mark the moss of many a hue
That varies the old tree's brown bark,
Or o'er the grey stone spreads.

The cluster'd berries claim the eye
O'er the bright hollies gay green leaves,
The ivy round the leafless oak
Clasps its full foliage close.

ROBERT SOUTHEY, FROM
'ODE WRITTEN ON THE FIRST OF DECEMBER'

# December 1

I set off this morning with an intention to go across the Weald to Worth; but the red rising of the sun and the other appearances of the morning admonished me to keep upon high ground; so I crossed the Mole, went along under Boxhill, through Betchworth and Buckland, and got to this place just at the beginning of a day of as heavy rain, and as boisterous wind, as, I think, I have ever known in England.

William Cobbett (1822)

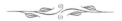

# December 2

I am going to detail all my troubles to you. In the first place, the door of my sitting-room doesn't quite fit, and a draught is the consequence. Secondly, there is a piano in the house which has decidedly entered on its second childhood, and this piano is occasionally played on by Miss P. with a really enviable *aplomb*. Thirdly, the knocks at the door startle me – an annoyance inseparable from a ground-floor room. Fourthly, Mrs P. scolds the servants *stringendo e fortissimo* while I am dressing in the morning. Fifthly – there is no fifthly.

George Eliot (1853)

# December 3

This morning is beautiful, and tempts me forth into the garden. It is all the walk that I can have at this season, but not all the exercise. I ring a peal every day upon the dumb-bells.

William Cowper (1785)

# December 4

A gusty wind makes the raindrops hit the window in stars, and the sunshine flaps open and shut like a fan, flinging into the room a tin-coloured light.

Thomas Hardy (1884)

# December 5

To-day there have come up from the country – not from my own home, which is too dry, but from near Salisbury – some branches cut from an old Thorn or Apple tree, and covered with long hoary-grey moss. I have put them into an old ginger-jar without water, and in this way they will last through the winter. They stand now against a red wall, where they look exceedingly well.

Mrs C. W. Earle (1896)

# December 6

I am filled to-night with a sense of gratitude. In this quiet parlour, on this foggy evening, by the cheerful candle-light, I have mused on my estate, which I see to be, in one sense, only 'a little lower than the angels'.

James Smetham (1853)

# December 7

Went to F— Duckponds. Flocks of Wigeon and Teal on the water. Taking advantage of a dip in the land managed to stalk them splendidly, and for quite a long time I lay among the long grass watching them through my field-glasses.

W. N. P. Barbellion (1906)

# December 8

I like a short journey in good company; and I like you all the better for your Englishman's humours. One doesn't find such things in London; something more like it here in the country, where every one, with whatever natural stock of intellect endowed, at least grows up his own way, and flings his branches about him, not stretched on the espalier of London dinner-table company.

Edward Fitzgerald (1844)

# December 9

A brilliant white frost and the hoary meadows sparkling with millions of rainbows and twinkling with diamonds.

Francis Kilvert (1873)

# December 10

Up, pretty well, the weather being become pretty warm again, and to the office, where we sat all the morning, and I confess having received so lately a token from Mrs Russell, I did find myself concerned for our not buying some tallow of her (which she bought on purpose yesterday most unadvisedly to her great losse upon confidence of putting it off to us). So hard it is for a man not to be warped against his duty and master's interest that receives any bribe or present, though not as a bribe, from any body else. But she must be contented, and I to do her a good turn when I can without wrong to the King's service. Then home to dinner (and did drink a glass of wine and beer, the more for joy that this is the shortest day in the year, which is a pleasant consideration) with my wife.

Samuel Pepys (1660)

# December 11

I mounted the 'Telegraph' at eight, and was in Keyhaven Cottage (just one hundred miles) within the twelve hours. But most wonderful and remarkably unfortunate, I had no sooner got about halfway on my journey down than my implacable enemy the weathercock flew into the west, and it began a hurricane and rain just as I entered the gig which took me from the coach at Lymington.

Colonel Peter Hawker (1829)

# December 12

There is a beauty in the trees peculiar to winter, when their fair delicate slender tracery unveiled by leaves and showing clearly against the sky rises bending with a lofty arch or sweeps gracefully drooping. The crossing and interlacing of the limbs, the smaller boughs and tender twigs make an exquisitely fine network which has something of the severe beauty of sculpture, while the tree in summer in its full pride and splendour and colour of foliage represents the loveliness of painting. The deciduous trees which seem to me most graceful and elegant in winter are the birches, limes, beeches.

Francis Kilvert (1874)

# December 13

Chill, frosty weather; such an atmosphere as forebodes snow in New England, and there has been a little here. Yet I saw a barefooted young woman yesterday. The feet of these poor creatures have exactly the red complexion of their hands, acquired by constant exposure to the cold air.

Nathaniel Hawthorne (1853)

# December 14

Bright Morn Frost rather harder, but not so severe to feel, use reconciling even this pleasant sensation. Cold has abated much of its fierceness to-day and seems inclined to relax a little; but will probably return again before noon.

Henry White (1784)

# December 15

Saw the limb of a rainbow footing itself on the sea at a small apparent distance from the shore, a thing of itself – no substrate cloud or even mist visible – but the distance glimmered through it as through a thin semi-transparent hoop.

Samuel Taylor Coleridge (1804)

I love to rise ere gleams the tardy light,
Winter's pale dawn; – and as warm fires illume,
And cheerful tapers shine around the room,
Thro' misty windows bend my musing sight
Where, round the dusky lawn, the mansions white,
With shutters clos'd, peer faintly thro' the gloom,
That slow recedes; while yon grey spires assume,
Rising from their dark pile, an added height
By indistinctness given. – Then to decree
The grateful thoughts to GOD, ere they unfold
To Friendship, or the Muse, or seek with glee
Wisdom's rich page! – O, hours! more worth than gold,
By whose blest use we lengthen Life, and free
From drear decays of Age, outlive the Old!

ANNA SEWARD, 'SONNET 40: DECEMBER MORNING'

# December 16

Brewed a Barrell of common Beer to day. Mr Symonds of Reepham, cleaned both my eight day Clocks to day, almost the whole day after them, he breakfasted & dined with our folks. When he went away, which was in the Evening I paid him a Bill for cleaning Clocks & Watch from October, 1789, to Dec. 1794 1.0.6 cleaning my Clocks to day included in it. I did not take any change of him out of a Guinea. Dinner to day, fine Rump of Beef boiled &c.

James Woodforde (1794)

# December 17

Snow in the night and still snowing... Ambleside looked excessively beautiful as we came out – like a village in another country; and the light cheerful mountains were seen, in the long distance, as bright and as clear as at mid-day, with the blue sky above them. We heard waterfowl calling out by the lake side. Jupiter was very glorious above Ambleside hills, and one large star hung over the corner of the hills on the opposite side of Rydale water.

Dorothy Wordsworth (1801)

# December 18

By the favour of the long dry weather I prevailed on Parsons to set-about cleansing the river course from Gracious-street to Webbs bridge, which was quite choak'd, & in great rains occasion'd a very troublesome flood. We threw out about 50 loads of mud, & have open'd so free a channel, that the road is quite dry, & the water will have an easy passage as fast as it comes to those parts.

Gilbert White (1762)

# December 19

Remember the pear trees in the lovely vale of Teme. Every season Nature converts me from some unloving heresy, and will make a Catholic of me at last.

Samuel Taylor Coleridge (1802)

# December 20

Finished plowing-up the Ewel-close, a wheat-stubble, to prepare it for barley, & grass-seeds: it must be plowed thrice. The ground is pretty dry, but tough, & heavy, requiring naturally much meliorating.

Gilbert White (1777)

# December 21

How beautiful a circumstance, the improvement of the flower, from the root up to that crown of its life and labours, that bridal-chamber of its beauty and its two-fold love, the nuptial and the parental – the womb, the cradle, and the nursery of the garden!

Samuel Taylor Coleridge (1804)

The radiant ruler of the year
At length his wintry goal attains;
Soon to reverse the long career,
And northward bend his steady reins.
Now, piercing half Potosi's height,
Prone rush the fiery floods of light
Ripening the mountain's silver stores:
While, in some cavern's horrid shade,
The panting Indian hides his head,
And oft the approach of eve implores.

But lo, on this deserted coast,
How pale the sun! how thick the air!
Mustering his storms, a sordid host,
Lo, Winter desolates the year.
The fields resign their latest bloom;
No more the breezes waft perfume,
No more the streams in music roll:
But snows fall dark, or rains resound;
And, while great Nature mourns around,
Her griefs infect the human soul.

MARK AKENSIDE, FROM 'ON THE WINTER-SOLSTICE'

# December 22

We breakfasted, dined, &c. again at home. Yesterday being Sunday & St Thomas's Day the Poor deferred going after their Christmas Gifts till this Morning, I had at my House fifty five, gave only to 53, the other two not living in the Parish. Gave in the Whole this Morn' at 6d each in Number 53 1.6.6. Dinner to day, boiled Beef & a rost Chicken... Very fine and open Weather for the Season. I cannot remember a finer day (I think) for St Thomas's Day, than this Day proved. Pray God! make us all thankfull for the same.

James Woodforde (1800)

# December 23

Before day. A lavender curtain with a pale crimson hem covers the east and shuts out the dawn.

Thomas Hardy (1873)

# December 24

I went to Chapel this Evening being Christmas Eve. I got into my own Rooms this Afternoon and there slept for the first Time – they are very good Rooms in the Lower Court, the second Stair Case next to the Chequer, one Pair of Stairs and the Door on the right Hand. Very wet, windy, and dismal Day.

James Woodforde (1773)

Christmas comes but once a year.
Though by nature snappy,
Let us, as we may, appear
Merry, friend, and happy!
Buckle to; and when you meet your
Thunderstricken fellow-creature,
Show the broad, indulgent smile
Of th' ingenuous crocodile!
Look as if you'd backed a winner!
Laugh, you miserable sinner!

Brother, Christmas Day has come.
Can't you seek for inspi-
ration in the turkey, plum-
pudding, beef, and mince-pie?
Brave it out, and tho' you sit on
Tenterhooks, remain a Briton;
You can only do your best;
Boxing Day's a day of rest!
Throw aside your small digestive
Eccentricities. Be festive!

Christmas Day is on the wing.
Are you feeling wroth with
Any one for anything?
Beg his pardon forthwith!
Though the right is all on your side,
Say it isn't; say 'Of course I'd
No intention – very rude –
Shocking taste –  but misconstrued'–
Then (while I admit it's horri-fying)
Tell the man you're sorry!

Christmas Day will soon have flown.
If, despite persuasion,
You resolve to be alone
On the glad occasion,
Better (do as I have done!)
Vanish with a scatter-gun;
If you have to see it through,
(Better do what I shall do!)
Dining quietly at the Club'll
Save us from a world of trouble!

JOHN KENDALL, 'CHRISTMAS GREETINGS'

# December 25

This is a most beautiful day of English winter; clear and bright, with the ground a little frozen, and the green grass along the waysides at Rock Ferry sprouting up through the frozen pools of yesterday's rain. England is forever green. On Christmas day, the children found wall-flowers, pansies, and pinks in the garden; and we had a beautiful rose from the garden of the hotel grown in the open air.

Nathaniel Hawthorne (1854)

How will it dawn, the coming Christmas Day?
A northern Christmas, such as painters love,
And kinsfolk, shaking hands but once a year,
And dames who tell old legends by the fire?
Red sun, blue sky, white snow, and pearled ice,
Keen ringing air, which sets the blood on fire,
And makes the old man merry with the young,
Through the short sunshine, through the longer night?
Or southern Christmas, dark and dank with mist,
And heavy with the scent of steaming leaves,
And rosebuds mouldering on the dripping porch;
One twilight, without rise or set of sun,
Till beetles drone along the hollow lane,
And round the leafless hawthorns, flitting bats
Hawk the pale moths of winter? Welcome then
At best, the flying gleam, the flying shower,
The rain-pools glittering on the long white roads,
And shadows sweeping on from down to down
Before the salt Atlantic gale: yet come
In whatsoever garb, or gay, or sad,
Come fair, come foul, 'twill still be Christmas Day.

CHARLES KINGSLEY, FROM 'CHRISTMAS DAY'

# December 26

With the dog for a walk around Windy Ash. It was a beautiful winter's morning – a low sun giving out a pale light but no warmth – a luminant, not a fire – the hedgerows bare and well trimmed, an Elm lopped close showing white stumps which glistened liquidly in the sun, a Curlew whistling overhead, a deeply cut lane washed hard and clean by the winter rains, a gunshot from a distant cover, a creeping Wren, silent and tame, in a bramble bush, and over the five-barred gate the granite roller with vacant shafts. I leaned on the gate and saw the great whisps of cloud in the sky like comets' tails. Everything cold, crystalline.

W. N. P. Barbellion (1911)

# December 27

Had 2 Bottles of my Wine.

James Woodforde (1759)

# December 28

Up at four in the morning, and afloat till five in the evening.
A dead calm, and the frost so hard that our beer froze up in
the bottles. Hot enough, however, what with thick clothing,
rowing, &c.

Colonel Peter Hawker (1829)

# December 29

The weather was beautiful yesterday, and the Queen had a
*long* drive and *walk*, which have done her great good; it is still
finer to-day.

Queen Victoria (1837)

# December 30

...On Thursday, 30th December, I went to Keswick. William rode before me to the foot of the hill nearest K. There we parted close to a little watercourse, which was then noisy with water, but on my return a dry channel. ...We stopped our horse close to the ledge, opposite a tuft of primroses, three flowers in full blossom and a bud. They reared themselves up among the green moss. We debated long whether we should pluck them, and at last left them to live out their day, which I was right glad of at my return the Sunday following; for there they remained, uninjured either by cold or wet.

Dorothy Wordsworth (1802)

# December 31

Edwin Law told me of an infallible receipt for warming cold and wet feet on a journey. Pour half a glass of brandy into each boot. Also he often carries a large pair of stockings with him to wear over boots and trousers.

Francis Kilvert (1874)

While snow the window-panes bedim,
　　The fire curls up a sunny charm,
Where, creaming o'er the pitcher's rim,
　　The flowering ale is set to warm;
　　Mirth, full of joy as summer bees,
　　Sits there, its pleasures to impart,
And children, 'tween their parent's knees,
　　Sing scraps of carols o'er by heart.

And some, to view the winter weathers,
　　Climb up the window-seat with glee,
Likening the snow to falling feathers,
　　In fancy infant ecstasy;
　　Laughing, with superstitious love,
O'er visions wild that youth supplies,
　　Of people pulling geese above,
And keeping Christmas in the skies.

As tho' the homestead trees were drest,
　　In lieu of snow, with dancing leaves,
As tho' the sun-dried martin's nest,
　　Instead of ickles, hung the eaves,
　　The children hail the happy day –
　　As if the snow were April's grass,
And pleas'd, as 'neath the warmth of May,
　　Sport o'er the water froze as glass.

JOHN CLARE, 'DECEMBER'

Have you enjoyed this book?
If so, why not write a review on your favourite website?

If you're interested in finding out more about our books
follow us on Twitter: **@Summersdale**

Thanks very much for buying this Summersdale book.

# www.summersdale.com